Beyond
Personal Development

Gert Jurg

Personal Development Series (complete):

The Enneagram in Personal Development (2016)

Life Phases in Personal Development (2018)

The ABC of Personal Development (2019)

Ascesis in Personal Development (2020)

Men and Women in Personal Development (2021)

Personal Development in the Western World (2022)

Beyond Personal Development (2023)

CONTENTS

PREFACE

It's 15 March 1345, a Wednesday. In Kalverstraat, Amsterdam, sixty-five-year-old Ysbrant Dommer feels so ill that he has a pastor come to his home. The priest gives the dying man a holy wafer and confers on him the sacrament of the sick. A short time after this, the man vomits up the wafer. To prevent desecration, his wife throws the vomit containing the Host in the fire, but the piece of consecrated bread remains unscathed and hovers above the burning fire. The Miracle of Amsterdam has come to pass.

The Miracle of the Host is quickly recognised by the municipality of Amsterdam and the Bishopric of Utrecht. Pilgrims soon flock from far and wide. A large pilgrimage chapel, de Heilige Stede (Holy Site), is erected where the house once stood. The Heiligeweg (Holy Way) becomes the principal pilgrimage path. In Kalverstraat today, on the corner of Wijde Kapelsteeg, one storey up, a small shrine can be found reading 'Gedachtenis ter Heilige Stede' (Remembrance to the Holy Site). This little monument, almost secretly, indicates the Holy Heart of Amsterdam.

Some decades before, at the beginning of the 14th century, Amsterdam was granted city rights and the combination of these two events, city rights and pilgrimage centre, prelude its growth towards the Golden Age metropolis of the 17th century. Amsterdam has always been a Catholic city at heart and remained so even after the Reformation when the Catholic faith was, for the next nearly 300 years, officially banned and informally tolerated by the Protestant authorities present. Hence the many stowed-away churches hidden behind everyday facades or disguised in attics.

Origin, heart and soul of my beloved metropole, this city I have lived and worked in for over thirty years, appears to be a living proof of the transubstantiation of the Body of Christ, initiating the solid establishment and miraculous development of this proud free state, harbour for the outcasts and the deprived, home for refugees and exiles and haven for free thinkers and free spirits. Tolerance, hospitality and adaptability have always been at the core of this vibrant society. Outwardly cherishing trade yet spiritually safeguarding life of soul.

The site where once the colossal Heilige Stede (Holy Site) was situated - covering one whole block - is now the domicile of the interactive, historical horror attraction The Amsterdam Dungeon. The smaller Reformed Church, that replaced its confiscated Catholic predecessor in 1912, has been traded and transformed into a multimedia spectacle about the bloody history of Amsterdam, performed by 7 actors in 11 shows. With such gloomy titles as 'The Torture Chamber' and 'The Spanish Inquisition', these shows focus on very different events than an ever-enlightening Eucharistic miracle.

However, a religious adventure has not become unfeasible in Amsterdam. One just has to be aware and open to the signs. I have my own Church Route through the centre of Amsterdam and it passes 15 churches in one hour, most of them of Catholic denomination and open for visit and prayer. Also in Kalverstraat and close to the Miracle Spot, we find, for example, a narrow alcove with a swing door, popularly referred to as De Papagaai (the Parrot Church), a concealed, intimate and artistically refined God house.

A long time ago, I lived for some years in the centre of Amsterdam, just behind Dam Square. From my bedroom, I could see the golden ornaments on top of the Royal Palace. All the way up, there's a sailing ship with two persons on board, complete with a flag and a rudder. Whenever I woke up, I had to adjust my lying position just a little to look at the slender boat and, when the sky happened to be blue, the golden vessel was shining brightly and hopefully.

While I was living there, I sometimes visited the chapel at Begijnhof, a tranquil oasis within the hectic swirl of the city. Although I didn't confess to any religion, I thoroughly appreciated the still and beneficent atmosphere inside the chapel. In this place I found it quite easy to enter into my meditation practice. Other guests and even tourists seemed to naturally respect the silence and sacredness. Even their whispering contributed to the sense of reverence and holiness. Also without faith or belief, one could relish a mystic presence.

This state of union, this sense of blurring boundaries, this feeling of deep connection, this experience of warmth and support, without knowing the people present or just completely on my own, is something I know from meditation groups, retreats and centres. Just being surrounded by people with the same intentions creates a harmonious field that simply feels so wonderful (until some well-meaning yet ignorant soul disturbs the peace). But alone, in a city, in a church, without a service, sensing this togetherness there, is a gift from the gods.

To submit to the authority of the world's religions has always been difficult for me. This applies to the Protestant religion I was brought up in, but also to other traditions, dogmas, texts and rituals. As soon as a doctrine takes over, the talking, the singing, the moving, the praying and the sharing lose their essential energy. That's how I feel. Without judging other people's experiences and beliefs in this area. Yet, in the openness of unknowingness, in the formless, is where I find a loving power from beyond.

I'm pushing an elephant up the stairs
I'm tossing out punchlines
That were never there
Over my shoulder a piano falls
Crashing to the ground

I'm breaking through
I'm bending spoons
I'm keeping flowers in full bloom
I'm looking for answers
From the great beyond

'The Great Beyond'
Man on the Moon
R.E.M., 1999

INTRODUCTION

Personal development happens in a context. A person does not live and work in isolation. There are connections. With family, friends, neighbours, colleagues and all people one meets in a lifetime. All of these connections together form a social network, a community, a society and, at large, the world. The world contains all other life forms too, as well as the material world including oceans, deserts, mountains and wilderness. The natural world is connected to the planetary world, the sheltering sky, the solar system, the milky way, the universe.

Coming to the end of the *Personal Development Series,* I present a book that goes beyond personal development. This may put some readers at guard. Is he writing about God? Is he speaking about our one and only Lord God? About mysticism? New Age? Spiritism? Universal Love? At this moment, I only want to say that we're all part of a whole, however we conceive this totality and whatever we think or feel about the possible connections to or influences from other parts of this vast and complex unity.

Whatever ideas you have in daily life about what is influencing your behaviour, your thoughts and your personal effectivity, whether it is your family, your education, the law, the weather, your mind, your heart, your soul or some benign and/or evil deity, the starting point here is that we all - each and every one of us - need some sort of Real-Life System, some understanding about cause and effect, some temporary idea of how everything is connected, to take the next step on our path of personal development.

Part of a whole. In this last book of the Series I will focus on what different world views and religions have to say about the composition and functioning of our world and humanity. Many terms and definitions are taken from Wikipedia. I will use all I know (naturally) and my knowledge and understanding are frightfully limited (obviously). Yet, I've been around and I am willing to engage in this lengthy conversation with you, yes you, about the way the world works and more. It may change your mind.

I know nothing about Jainism, Rastafari, Mormonism and Australian Aboriginal Religion and Mythology, just to mention a few. I may someday be converted to the Baha'i Faith, Zoroastrianism or some form of folk religion, but I don't know that now. I dare to assert that I have a general understanding of the principal world views and world religions. All of my life, I have had an innate curiosity about how people think, what they believe, how they know what they say they know and what may improve their lives.

To the staunch atheist, I would like to say: I am not a representative of any fixed belief system. To the convinced humanist, I would like to say: my aim is to challenge your belief system. To the secular Buddhist, I would like to say: open your mind to the unknown forces in the universe. To the traditional Muslim and the orthodox Christian, I would like to say: could it be that various belief systems carry the message of Jesus and the Prophet wearing another cloth? You're all invited.

During my years in the Ridhwan School, a modern approach to spiritual development, the subject of God and religion was addressed in a seminar entitled 'The Beyond'. The big group of 150 people was divided into small groups according to the denomination that they were brought up in. Among these were a group of Catholics, several groups of competing Protestants, a group of atheists and a group of hippies and new age. It was astounding how much fun and recognition this temporary get-together raised. It felt like coming home.

Many wars have been fought and are still fought in the name of God. Bob Dylan wrote a chilling song about this phenomenon, 'With God on Our Side'. Having arrived in my sixtieth year of life, I feel the monopolisation of 'the beyond' is the greatest threat to world peace. My deepest desire in life is to embrace each and every world view, faith and truth within an unspeakable unity. In awe of that, this book is my last effort, within this Series, to help create a common humanity.

I very much like this word, 'beyond', capitalised or not, for it points in a direction without prescribing what one should or could find there. An inviting openness towards the unknown is implied. I also very much like the R.E.M.-song 'The Great Beyond', lyrics partly printed before. The Great Spirit - the term from the Native American tradition that refers to the Great Mystery - inspires me, makes me joyful, animated and thankful. Many people have their own favourite name for their conception, experience or feeling of the beyond.

I have a special connection with the poet Rainer Maria Rilke. It is as if his words resonate with a truth that lies in my heart. Whenever I read his lines, I feel an even deeper layer of truth may be opened in me, a depth that surprises me yet is instantly recognised as being intrinsically mine. I am astonished that a man living a century ago can feel so near and well-attuned. It makes me wonder about time and space and, with Rilke, about the nature of God.

GERT JURG

What will you do, God, when I die?
I am your jar (if cracked, I lie?)
Your well-spring (if the well go dry?)
I am your craft, your vesture I —
You lose your purpose, losing me.

When I go, your cold house will be
Empty of words that made it sweet.
I am the sandals your bare feet
Will seek and long for, wearily.

Your cloak will fall from aching bones.
Your glance, that my warm cheeks have cheered
As with a cushion long endeared,
Will wonder at a loss so weird;
And, when the sun has disappeared,
Lie in the lap of alien stones.

What will you do, God? I am feared.

'Was wirst du tun, Gott, wenn ich sterbe?'
Rainer Maria Rilke, *Das Stunden-Buch*, 1905
Translation A. Yarmolnksy & B. Deutsch
Published in *Poetry*, edition December 1922

A TEACHING THAT HEALS

Seven years ago, I published my first book, titled *The Enneagram in Personal Development*. After twenty-odd years of working with the system of the enneagram, I felt I could contribute something valuable to and missing in the existing contemporary literature on the subject. And I did. In the intervening years, peers, clients and laymen praised my unique approach to the matter which concentrated on the transformational potential of the system. I presented the enneagram as a psychological and spiritual typology that distinguishes nine (*ennea* in Greek) types of people.

A typology, that is how the enneagram - spilled over from America - has been popularised in Europe since the nineties. It has proven to be very useful as a typology, both in the business world and in the area of personal growth. Nowadays, many psychology curricula treat this model by default, especially since its favourable scientific evaluation and assessment at Stanford University. From my first introduction to this oracle of wisdom, I knew however that its meaning, depth and range go far beyond a simple and insightful typology.

Russian philosopher P.D. Ouspensky was among the first to write about the enneagram. His book *In Search of the*

Miraculous: Fragments of an Unknown Teaching was posthumously published in 1949 yet conceived much earlier, during his apprentice years with Armenian mystic G.I. Gurdjieff, between 1914 and 1924. Gurdjieff distinguished his so-called 'Fourth Way' from the way of bodily struggle (the way of the fakir), the way of purification of the emotions (the way of the monk) and the way of purification of the mind (the way of the yogi).

The Fourth Way affects all aspects of man at the same time and it requires no renunciation or belief. It can be and indeed must be practiced in the midst of ordinary life conditions. Ouspensky writes about the hidden origin and the application of the enneagram. 'This symbol cannot be met with anywhere in the study of 'occultism', either in books or in oral transmission. It was given such significance by those who knew that they considered it necessary to keep the knowledge of it secret.' (1949, pg. 294).

He adds (1949, pg. 301) that '... it must be understood that the enneagram is a universal symbol. All knowledge can be included in the enneagram and with the help of the enneagram it can be interpreted. And in this connection only what a man is able to put into the enneagram does he actually know, that is, understand. What he cannot put into the enneagram he does not understand. For the man who is able to make use of it, the enneagram makes books and libraries entirely unnecessary.'

'Everything can be included and read in the enneagram. A man may be quite alone in the desert and he can trace the enneagram in the sand and in it read the eternal laws of the universe. And every time he can learn something new, something he did not know before.' 'The enneagram is the fundamental hieroglyph of a universal language which has as many different meanings as there are levels of men.' It is quite something to say about a popular character topology chatted about in *Marie Claire*.

This information I couldn't present in my first book as its sole purpose there was to clarify the transformational potential of the nine types of people. Yet, having arrived at the seventh and last book of the Series, I come back to the system I described in the first book, to broaden its scope, specify its meaning and deepen its understanding. In fact, taking the enneagram as an entrance to a totality of ideas that unfolded in the subsequent parts of the Series, I have already employed its essence.

Furthermore, my knowledge of and experience with the enneagram has developed during the last seven years. The reason I am starting this book with an advanced description of the enneagram is that I gradually began to feel its healing power. For practically thirty years, I thought of the enneagram as a system of knowledge that could easily and profoundly be applied in the field of coaching and consultancy. Recently, I have come to see that the essential enneagram is more like a system of medicine, like Ayurveda or TCM.

In reductionist Western thinking, we tend to separate the mind from the body. In more holistic approaches like Traditional Chinese Medicine and Shamanic Healing, this separation is unthinkable, unsubstantiated and unproductive. Unaware and ignorant as I was all those years, I just viewed the enneagram as this huge vessel of knowledge. However, in the process of helping people find their type and applying its potential for personal growth, I, step by step, began to actually feel its warm, connecting and mysterious healing power. This has been an astounding revelation.

I must add that I am not up to date with the enneagram literature from about the last decade. So maybe other 'enneagrammists' have, in the meantime, written about this matter too. In my thirty years of enneagram work, I have not come across this notion. Yet, again, I may have been blind to its presence, occurrence and appearance. What's more important, my 'revelation' has revived my interest in and work with the enneagram. I would like to share a few things about this. For example, what is healing?

I wish to distinguish between the *process* of healing and the *result* or *effect* of healing. These are both difficult matters to discuss because it is hard to describe the process objectively as well as to actually measure its outcome. I can only recount what happens with me and with my clients during my consultations. We start with knowledge, transmission and understanding but then something deeper enters the equation. It can best be described as a warm, helping, energetic presence that comes into the room, felt by us both.

This warm, gentle presence is not a ghost, nor do we penetrate a spiritualistic or occult dimension. There are no tables moving; there's nothing dark or frightening about this phenomenon. I can only say that it feels like the enneagram has its own (invisible) spirit or angel or atmosphere. One can sense this presence, even describe its working and effect but one has no direct contact with its source. Yet, it is real, sensible and sometimes tangible. It's something like a *deva*, as Ayurvedic medicine has its deity, Dhanvantari.

My assumption is that the system called the enneagram, like the Eastern medicine systems mentioned, has its own spiritual force or being or guardian angel behind or within its nature. When the facilitator working with such a system is attuned to its nature, the presence of its power becomes perceptible. In fact, it starts to cooperate, or maybe better said: it joins in. This reminds me of the joke about the elephant and the mouse on the bridge, where the mouse says: how good are we stomping together, hey!

For, who is leading the show now? Me, a well-meaning counsellor, in a small workspace in an outskirt of Amsterdam, Holland? Or the eternal wisdom of an omnipotent presence far beyond my perception and understanding, the power behind the throne? Anyway, the session continues and, at the end, my client feels much better, not only more knowledgeable or proficient in application but touched on the level of heart and soul. After this encouraging moment, it's impossible, in hindsight, to determine what the effect has been on the client's life.

Thus, after many years of envisioning the enneagram as a wise teacher, I now envision the enneagram as a potential power of healing. With the image of the latter, it's my task as a facilitator to attune to this energy source, to find the right attitude in myself to approach this helping hand, not too demanding but not too timid either. I must know my place. That's probably a case of maturation, perhaps even a matter of age. If one serves well long enough, one is granted a promotion.

And thus, to start and to end the Series with this profound and comprehensive model of the world, and all that is in it, seems to create a sound and sturdy container for all that has been said in book I to VI and for all that still will be said in this edition, book VII. As I indicated, next year I will have worked and lived with the enneagram for thirty years, with it having a central place in my thinking, doing and being. I love the enneagram.

THINGS IN HEAVEN AND EARTH

Readers familiar with my work know that I treasure to quote Shakespeare, especially from Hamlet. Here we go again... 'There are more things in heaven and earth, Horatio, / Than are dreamt of in your philosophy.' This could be considered the starting point for our exploration in this book. This will be and must be a personal survey or inquiry. We are entering the domain of the metaphysical, the subjective, the mystical. In this respect, I must ask for your patience. Especially if you like quick and actionable solutions.

At some point in the chapters to come, some of you may feel we are getting hopelessly lost. What has this got to do with that, you may wonder. What has the following to do with the previous, you may ask in despair. What have these notions to do with <u>my</u> personal development, you may exclaim in irritation. Please restrain your impatience. I promise you, everything will fall into place towards the end. What I will be doing, in the meantime, is to rake the ground of your consciousness.

Modern man, specifically Western man, has lost their sense of the magical, the invisible, the supernatural. We've been raised within a straitjacket of restrictive rationality and anything that does not fit in this model is dismissed as made-up, fantasy or superstition. When a young child has an imaginary friend, for example, its parents quickly and lovingly relegate this story to the realm of fiction. Out of kindness, we may tolerate such an anomaly for some time, yet we are sure such a thing doesn't really exist. Or does it?

Young children sometimes talk about meeting a dead grandparent, whether or not recently deceased. While we may smilingly or cautiously take the time to listen to our loved ones, we are thinking about how to explain that such a meeting cannot really happen and is not really true. Many a child is sad and lost when they find out that Santa Claus is in fact a fabrication. When I was told, at the appropriate age, that Santa didn't exist, I naturally assumed that God would be next in line.

Jules Verne had to promise his parents that he would only travel in his imagination. He did and wrote all these lovely, adventurous books. I feel a sharp pain deep down in my belly, even writing this down now. It's like a physical amputation to me, the thought of a child who is forbidden to consider its imagination being a reality. Archangels and guardian angels, gnomes in the garden, witches and fairies, wizards and magicians; many people, and not only children, see them, hear them and talk to them.

What is not taken from us as toddlers is suppressed in our minds when we enter the school system. The left hemisphere is favoured over the right hemisphere. The rational, analytical mind is considered superior to the creative, intuitive mind. We learn how to write abstract letters, how to construct words and sentences. This we recognise as the language spoken at home. Besides letters, we learn numbers and arithmetic. We are taught how to count in a decimal system, how to add and subtract, how to divide and multiply.

Some school systems are aware of this one-sidedness. In Waldorf and Montessori education, a better balance is achieved between the rational-analytical and the creative-intuitive. Yet, these schools are also subject to standardised attainment targets. Our democracies exercise stern control as to what its future grown-up inhabitants are supposed to know and who they are to be. Primary schools deliver their manufactures to secondary schools and secondary schools perfect the semi-finished products, ready for further vocational education and universities. Hardly anyone can escape this elaborate and sophisticated order of socialisation.

The same spell is cast against religious awareness. The strict separation in truthfulness between the rational and irrational and the physical and meta-physical is also applied to the natural and supernatural as well as to the earthly and heavenly empires. Thor and Wotan are inventions of our scared and ignorant Germanic predecessors, just like the Greeks made up Zeus and Athena and the Romans devised Jupiter and Minerva. From there it is a small step to question the divine authenticity of Jewish Yahweh, Islamic Allah and the Christian Jesus.

Of course, I respect anyone's godless universe, yet I often feel that an artificial and unneeded separation is made between the rational and the mystical, between the mind and the heart. Then two currents are created, two parties. Both parties think that the other is at least mistaken, but often they feel the others are misled, brainwashed or just plain stupid. Buses drive through the centres of London and Amsterdam carrying the slogan 'There's probably no God' while billboards proclaim, 'Jesus loves you'. Can we find a middle ground?

When I was fourteen, I lost my faith. Before, I had the conviction that God was God as the Bible and the Church professed. But around my puberty I started thinking about this and I didn't feel, didn't experience a connection with whatever could fall in this category, 'God'. This made me sad. Surrounded by friends and in a cultural climate that mocked the whole business of religion, I had no reason to question my position and joined the intellectual choir that ditched the concept of any supreme being.

This process continued and intensified during my years in college. My peer group was more interested in existentialism and socialism. I also liked Eastern philosophy. With a friend, I joined a yoga-class and through movement and breathing exercises and meditation techniques I felt deeper into myself and came in contact with a wider inner space. This felt great and personal and true. After class, our yoga teacher, on our request, taught us about Hinduism, Indian Gods and the ancient Vedas. There was something magical and appealing about this all.

What happened, I think now in retrospect, is that, in this case, my inner experience went hand in hand with the knowledge, insights and stories that were provided. Back home in church, I had never felt any personal connection with what was read, taught, sung and preached. But that didn't mean that my connection with the supernatural, with the mystery or, if you want, with God, was absent or destroyed. I only missed the right words to see my inner experience reflected in the religious language of my time.

I had just been missing a teacher, a wise elder, a spiritual mentor. There was a void, yet my inner 'beingness' was open, attuned and, if you want, believing. Through Hinduism and Buddhism I found the reflection of my inner spirituality. Also, as a student, I came across the work of psychiatrist Carl Gustav Jung, a colleague of Sigmund Freud, who expanded his work on depth psychology. Jung wrote about mysticism and Christianity in a manner that I could relate to. And in this way, I reconnected with Christianity.

Through the inner work, the inner feeling of my own breath, awareness, soul and self, I reconnected to this void place inside of me that I recognised as essentially religious. I realised that this holy space had always been inside me, mostly wordless, sometimes flickering as a light, often just dark and still. In time I began to see that spiritual and religious awareness are two inner realms, close to one another, similar, and yet to be distinguished. The spiritual being more immanent and the religious being more transcendent.

If someone asks me now 'Do you believe in God?', I have a few answers. People, particularly in the West and especially in Holland, want to know what category to place you in. Do you believe in God or not? Are you with us or are you with them? Like in the States, whether you are a Republican or a Democrat. Sometimes I answer, 'I don't believe in God, I walk with God'. This could be taken as blasphemous by the orthodox Christian, for only Enoch walked with God.

Sometimes I say, 'I have a wide-ranging religious interest'. Sometimes I say, 'I believe in the unity of all religion'. It all depends on the one who asks. Still, all three of these answers are honest. During the day, I bring my attention back to a holy place within me, a place where I sometimes sense a Holy Presence, like being with a really good friend, my Beloved, the Supreme Absolute. I sense the beyond in inner stillness or in human contact, in the mountain or in the winds.

I AM PART OF THE BEAUTY

I tried to think of some way
To let my face become his.

'Could I whisper in your ear
a dream I've had? You're the only one
I've told this to.'

He tilts his head, laughing,
as if, 'I know the trick you're hatching,
but go ahead.'

I am an image he stitches with gold thread
on a tapestry, the least figure,
a playful addition.

But nothing he works on is dull.
I am part of the beauty.

Rumi (translation C. Barks)
Poem No '40'
These Branching Moments, 1988

In my years as a student at the Ridhwan School, I was introduced to the poetry of Rumi, Jalal al-Din Rumi, the great 13th century Sufi master. During talks, his poems (in an English translation) were read out loud to elucidate the spiritual teachings that were transmitted. I was so touched by his lines that I spontaneously started to compose music to his poetry. This in itself was a spiritual experience. I felt his 800-year-old wisdom pass through me while singing his radiant rhyme to a brand-new conceived melody.

Music was my first love and it will be my last. At eight years old, I ran around the table in the living room, singing along with 'Wig-Wam Bam', a pop song by seventies British glam rock band The Sweet. It was my first vinyl single record. When I was ten, I sang along phonetically, headphones on, with *Sgt. Pepper's Lonely Hearts Club Band* from The Beatles. At the age of twelve, I set up a four-boy playback band and 'played' my first gig at our school farewell party.

At my secondary school farewell party, I was now 18 years old, I performed with a real rock band, playing our own songs and singing my own lyrics. Meanwhile, I'd been classically trained on the piano and after that had a teacher who taught me free improvisation. From then on, I wrote my own songs but didn't perform often. Not until 2001, at 37, did I begin to record the music I had gathered through the years. Also the Rumi songs found their way to studio recorded music albums.

All over the world, sacred and religious texts have been handed down the centuries by singing, chanting and reciting. Incredibly sizeable texts have been passed down from generation to generation in this way. The ancient Hindu poems Ramayana and Mahabharata began as stories told through oral tradition which scholars believe predates their first written versions by almost one thousand years. Note, the Ramayana consists of some 24,000 verses and the Mahabharata contains even 100,000 verses. Reciting in metric is easier to remember, but it is still an unbelievable feat!

In religious rituals, it is common to have music accompanying ancient texts. A quarter of the Dutch still visit a church every week and there is a lot of singing there. It's not only about the transmission of content, remembrance through repetition, it's also about sensing the community, the feeling of togetherness, the expressive participation in the ceremonies and praising and honouring deities. Religious singing is a form of prayer, worship and reverence. Think also of lavish hallelujah services and frenzied evangelicals! You can love them or hate them.

The Sufi tradition, wherein Rumi stands, knows a special kind of music and dance called Sufi whirling or turning and is performed by Sufi dervishes of the Mevlevi order (and other orders). Sufism is generally considered to be the third branch of Islam, alongside Sunni and Shia. The whirling dervishes engage in an exhilarating meditation practice through which they aim to reach the source of all perfection. This is sought by abandoning one's ego, by listening to matching music, focusing on God and spinning one's body in repetitive circles.

The music I've composed to the poems of Rumi, beautifully translated by the American Coleman Barks, as well as to the poems of Hafez, a 14th century Persian poet, just as beautifully translated by the American Daniel Ladinsky, has given me a special entrance to the rich content of the verses. I can always sing these songs to inspire, comfort and uplift me. I sometimes hear them being played in my mind (or heart) as if I am being reminded not to lose hope. The Friend is always around.

My love for Sufism was intensified through my visit to Konya, the hometown of Rumi in Turkish Anatolia. On the high-speed train from Istanbul to Konya I talked with a friendly and knowledgeable local Quran teacher who ran a boy's school. Rumi's mausoleum is situated in the local Mevlâna Museum. Mevlâna is his honorary title, meaning 'master'. The sanctuary has a very gentle atmosphere. Sufism treats men and women alike and I had the impression

I could feel that and notice it in the attitude of the women present.

On a regular Saturday, I tried to attend a Whirling Dervish performance (or *sema*) at the Mevlâna Cultural Centre on the outskirts of Konya but, when I was there, the stadium-size site was all desolate and deserted. Neither my taxi driver nor my hotelier knew what was going on. Maybe it was not yet my time. A few years later, I was invited to a traditional Turkish wedding on the outskirts of Amsterdam and totally unexpected a Whirling Dervish performed his mesmerising and energising spin. I was deeply moved.

Sufism helps me to honour the horizontal dimension of spirituality too, by which I mean that God is presented as the Friend and the Beloved. God is walking beside me. He is available and kind and supportive, to be felt, enjoyed and experienced. Many poems by Rumi have a sensual tone, they radiate warmth, speak of sensual love, yet without any trace of questionable or vulgar sexuality. The body is allowed in Sufism. Sufism does not advocate the so-called *via negativa*, the path of renunciation, of leaving the world.

On the contrary, the *via affirmative* is embraced whereby true happiness is found not by rejecting the world but by plunging into it and instead of getting lost in its dazzling splendours, finally rejoicing in and joining forces with its underlying oneness. Personally and from a stern Calvinistic background, I have a penchant for silence, meditating on my own, a monastic life. Rumi invites me to come out and play, to love and be loved, to participate and celebrate life, to hurt and cry, to fall and rise again.

My Ridhwan teachers also recited poems by Rainer Maria Rilke, from *The Book of Hours* (*Das Stunden-Buch*, 1905). Speaking German, I could not only compose music to the English translations but also to the original verses. Coleman Barks' first book (1988) quotes Rilke. From its Introduction: 'When the greatest spiritual poet of this century, Rainer Maria Rilke, saw the Mevlevi dervishes in Cairo on December 17, 1910, he wrote: "It is so truly the mystery of

the kneeling of the deeply kneeling man… which is celebrated in this night.'"

> From the beginning of my life
> I have been looking for your face
> but today I have seen it
>
> Today I have seen
> the charm, the beauty,
> the unfathomable grace
> of the face
> that I was looking for
>
> Today I have found you
>
>
> Rumi (translation F. Kia)
> 'Looking for Your face'
> *The Love Poems of Rumi*, 1998

FIFTY SHADES OF PRAYER

When I was in my teens and twenties, I found it difficult to pray. There's nothing out there to pray to, so why
fold your hands, close your eyes and murmur some silly
wishes into an empty universe? I still often feel this way
when I pray. I don't experience a deity anywhere near; I
don't 'believe' a priori a supreme being exists. As I mentioned earlier, I did find solace in meditation, discovered
an inner space, an inner centre and an inner peace. But not
always, for sure.

Yet something has happened during my forty years of
meditation practice. Concentrating on the breath, the belly
centre (*kath* or *chi* point) or my inner beingness, sometimes
a special sensation joins the party. If you have never felt
this, it may be difficult to follow. Meditation evokes the
inner observer; you becomes a witness to whatever goes
on in your awareness, be it thoughts, feelings or body sen-
sations. And at some point, you, being the monitor, know
what's going on. You learn to recognise the truth of your
experience.

This knowing is beyond naming, labelling and interpreting. It is knowing because you know when you know
that you know. And this is not circular reasoning. When

you feel love, you know it is love. There's no doubt about it. When you feel sadness, you know it is sadness. As you are developing your skill of knowing what you are experiencing, you become more sophisticated in this art. Some people call this process 'understanding'. The trick is not to make things up. You wait for the knowing to arise.

In this way, I have learned (for myself) to recognise a unique sensation which sometimes comes up in meditation. It's a very special sense of subtlety. It feels expectant. The energy is warm and hopeful and uplifting. There is an immediate sense of carefulness, not fear. A knowing that one has to be very attentive with something so valuable. When I focus on this sensation, this energy field, a sense of holiness, of reverence, of awe, comes with it. I become very still with this presence. I feel blessed.

There's an invitation that comes from such an experience which is to focus on its presence. While meditation for me is an opening, a perceiving, a registering, this special experience calls for active aiming, focusing and conscious connecting. At a certain moment, I know that this is prayer. I may also sense an invitation and then an urge to speak, albeit in silence. All this time, there's no will to label the source of focus and invitation. It's just there in all its gentle might, a patiently awaiting presence.

By gaining some experience with this process, you learn to distinguish different aspects of prayer. It is important to mention here that there is no coercion or temptation whatsoever. Only a possibility is offered. You may disconnect at any time and, for example, return to 'normal' meditation or to your daily activities. What's more, it is important to say that the whole happening is light-hearted, simple and plain, no hocus-pocus. The nearness of greatness always makes me want to put my palms together if not to fold my hands.

Playing with this mode of meditation and inner inquiry, I have learned many different ways and aspects of praying. This experiment has crystallised in a threefold 'approach' which I still vary and adjust and explore. I am presenting my own experience just as an example, not as a guideline or precept. If you feel drawn to experiment in this field of consciousness yourself, you will surely find your own style. My personal threefold way consists of A. to Praise (thank), B. to Propose (ask) and C. to Perceive (listen).

I have found that it feels pleasant to begin a prayer with gratitude and appreciation. And that's how I called phase A for a long time. However, there is an ancient tradition of praise when praying. Praise the Lord! After much hesitation and with great difficulty, I tried that approach. And behold, it has become joyful. Start with the positive. Count your blessings. Realise how much you have and how much goes well in your life. Thank existence, life, the universe or God for all good things of today.

Next, propose. This may concern a special request or a dedication. You can commend a matter or a person to all good forces in beingness. I use the word 'propose' to imply that I am asking for special attention for something. I am presenting a proposal and I leave it entirely to the discretion of 'the other side' as to what to do with my proposal. I think that's fair. Thy Will Be Done. This is what is commonly understood by praying: asking for help, especially with urgent ego-concerns.

If praying is a quiet, daily ritual for which you take all the time needed, there is less pressure on phase B, both in form and content. Which brings us to the often-neglected phase C, perceive or listen. In our Western history of religion, there isn't much talk of Providence returning the call. The impression we get is of the transcendent God mostly keeping quiet. At least in the last centuries in, for example, the Abrahamic religions, Judaism, Christianity and Islam. God doesn't talk back, it is generally assumed.

If someone in our direct vicinity would claim that God is speaking to them in person, we would at least frown and be cautious. Some people would discard such testimony immediately and would call in the infirmaries! Yet, in the stillness of a private meditation, it is very well possible to receive encouragement, when 'Mother Mary comes to me', as Paul McCartney shared, 'speaking words of wisdom, let it be'. It is certainly possible to hear or perceive the right words spoken, to receive an answer to your prayer.

It's just a very subtle matter and a very private and very intimate affair. The easier, firmer and louder people proclaim that they know what is said or wanted from the other side, the less likely it is that they are relying on the right 'voice'. Many people, from all walks of life, know precisely what I mean and work with this daily. It's just a matter that is almost too precious and too delicate to discuss here on paper. I only want to say, be still and listen.

Over the years I have experimented with all kinds of prayers, much to my own shame and delight. There is dedicating prayer, there is pleading prayer, there is crying prayer, there is desperate prayer, there is aggrieved prayer, there is joyful prayer, there is ecstatic prayer. There is long prayer and short prayer. There is light prayer and heavy prayer. There is grateful prayer and devoted prayer. There is praying for something small and praying for something grand. There is the death prayer and there is the last prayer.

You have probably noticed that I have hitherto carefully avoided the issue of answered prayer. But it seems not unfair to put forward the issue of the effectivity of prayer. Does it help? Do I get what I ask for? Why else would I bother? I'm investing all this time and effort in this activity and I want to see some results, for God's sake! Give some, get some, y'know what I mean?! The funny thing is that prayer does work but not if you put it like this.

What happens in ongoing inner contact with the transcendent dimension is that a deeper understanding of the ways of the world is forged. You start to feel what is possible and what is not. You start to sense what is just and what is selfish. In time this inner dialogue makes you wiser, more distinctive about the nature of your desires. Comfort comes from praying itself, not from a specific outcome.

You are growing up. You no longer hand in your wish list to Santa Claus. Your actions evolve.

To aid his personal development, a friend of mine employed this question for a long time: What stands between me and God now? He worked with this question daily and tried to be aware what thoughts and feelings came up. He carried a constant reminder of his deepest wish in life with him. His question became a mantra and his inquiry became a prayer. His prayer became a way of life, a way of walking. He walked with his question and one day God joined him as he walked.

GO AND REPAIR MY HOUSE

If you take the path down just outside the Porta Nuova in Assisi in Italy, you come to a chapel with a small monastery, San Damiano. It is an exquisite sanctuary where, in 1205, according to Franciscan sources, Giovanni di Pietro di Bernardone, also known as Saint Francis, heard an exhortation from Christ. Kneeling in prayer before the image of the Crucifix, he heard a voice descend to him from the cross, saying three times: Go, Francis, and repair my house which, as you see, is all in ruins!

In 2019, I stayed for a week in Assisi in what happened to be the coldest May month ever recorded. Because of it, there were hardly any tourists around. Normally, and I had witnessed this once myself, the place is packed, swarmed with day trippers from Rome and Florence, released into the fragile town, each day and all day, by dozens of coaches and touring cars. This time, I could easily imagine myself walking around in mediaeval times, pulling my hood tight over my head against the drizzling rain.

San Damiano is one of my favourite spots in Assisi. I took the trip down and up again once a day or so. It felt like a concise pilgrimage. Meditating in this little chapel is very special if you're lucky enough not to be disturbed by coat crackling, sack creaking, wacko whispering tourons. I still have to work on my patience and anger, I know. And this was even a quiet period! But the energy in this sanctuary is so beautiful, so gentle, so precious, so nourishing, so sacred.

Saint Francis took action to actually repair the structure of the San Damiano church although he eventually realised that God's message to him was to restore the entire Catholic Church as a whole body rather than literally repair one stone structure. Santa Chiara, Francis' soul mate and religious compeer, died in this monastery and in a small hut in the garden, Francis, in total seclusion and deathly ill, composed his famous poem *The Canticle of the Sun*. It is believed to be among the first works in Italian literature.

Since my first arrival in Assisi, thirty years ago, Francis had begun to follow me around. With my then-girlfriend, I attended a classical concert in the Upper Basilica and I was indescribably touched while my girlfriend could not stop crying. When we arrived at her family in Belgium on the way back, we stumbled across a man-sized statue of Saint Francis in the hallway. My mother kept a postcard we sent with the *Prayer of Saint Francis* (which is actually not his!) in her bible for all these years.

Walking up and down the small town to and from the Basilica again in 2019, I felt like a mediaeval monk. This time I was alone in Assisi, had seen all the sites, could not stretch out lazy in the Umbrian sun and so I was sent on an inner journey, to assess where I was and where I was going. I could sit for hours in the Basilica of Saint Clare, near to my hotel, looking at an altarpiece depicting Christ's Descent from the Cross, close to tears.

In yet another church, I ran into a Franciscan friar and could finally ask him what had been on my mind for a long time. Franciscans carry a rope as a belt around their waist keeping their habit tight and one end of this rope, swaying when walking, holds three knots. I always imagined these three knots would symbolise the three Franciscan precepts, obedience, poverty and chastity, as a constant reminder, like a knot in one's handkerchief. This Franciscan monk smiled surprised. He'd never thought nor heard of this!

Close to Assisi, Francis had built himself a small hut, near the chapel of Porziuncola, and there he died. I meditated on the exact spot. According to legend, he stripped naked and stretched out on the bare soil, flat on his face. At home, I bought a booklet with the collected writings of Saint Francis, which isn't a lot. Some references are (admittedly) questionable, but the simple and direct words of the master himself radiate a plainness and purity that bring me to silence, evoking a calm, earnest sincerity.

I have never been much of a Jesus fan. To quote Michael Stipe, lyricist of rock band R.E.M.: I can't say that I love Jesus/ That would be a hollow claim/ He did make some observations/ And I'm quoting them today ('New Test Leper', 1996). I learned to pray to Jesus when I was a child, but when I reached the age of discretion, I started to feel dishonest. At that time I saw the rock opera *Jesus Christ Superstar* which I loved and could totally sing along to.

I have a much deeper connection to Francis of Assisi, although, funny enough, this man, himself often referred to as The Second Christ, constantly points to Jesus! I know that Jesus is a historical figure. Roman politician Tacitus (c. AD 56 - c. 120) reports that Jesus was executed while Pontius Pilate was the Roman prefect in charge of Judaea. Yet, the figure of Jesus, the person, the accounts, the imagery, the character if you want, never spoke to me. While I even composed music to his Sermon on the Mount!

At secondary school we used to nickname everyone, often choosing the most horrible expressions which I am afraid to repeat. My own nickname was The Reverend and maybe I came up with it myself. Apparently, I preached a lot back then too! Or I thought I knew everything and had to advise everyone. Many years later, I organised a church service with a friend of mine which was both serious and hilarious. Under the title 'Laughing with God', we personified two extravagant Protestant reverends before a congregation of friends.

In my family there are Christians, atheists and agnostics. Being the youngest, I always felt, even from a young age, it was up to me to bring everyone together, to connect all apparently mutually exclusive truths. A hopeless task! I seemed to think that by explaining one's truth to another person, I would help them understand each other better and, in this way, could create peace. I think I am still trying to do that, but now beyond my family, as a counsellor, as a teacher, as a writer.

I like to go to churches. In Amsterdam, in Assisi and beyond. For a moment of quiet time, to meditate or pray, to light a candle for a loved one, to join a service or to sing out loud the psalms and hymns I grew up with. Catholic churches are of course filled to the brim with imagery of Jesus Christ. For years now, for decades, all my life really, I have looked, I have stared, I have gazed at paintings, icons and statues of Jesus. Without a connection.

Over the last seven years, I have participated in annual Christmas week retreats in various Benedictine monasteries throughout Holland. I have loved the chanting, I have loved the rituals, I have loved the stillness. Though I have not spoken much with the monks and laymen present at these retreats, I assume that they all deeply worship Christ. Yet, 'faith is a gift... that I have yet to receive', to quote Tom Hanks in his role as Robert Langdon in the movie *Angels & Demons* (2009). Am I holding back?

Let me be clear. I am not looking for conversion. I am not complaining about a lack of repentance or a missing faith. I am completely satisfied with what I think, feel and experience. I am also not secretly trying to say that there's really nothing to believe in, that Jesus as Christ does not exist or that all believers are ignorant blockheads. I am not jealous either. Well, yes, maybe sometimes, a little. Envious of the certainty that some faithful radiate, whatever their creed. But not really, actually.

It's an open matter, as far as I'm concerned. At deepest, I am curious to discover the truth about myself, about my place and direction in this world, about my service and contribution to humanity. I try to register, to observe, to witness. I try not to fill in the gaps. Each morning, I bow to Saint Francis, to a replica of a fresco (allegedly but disputed) by Giotto, from the Upper Basilica in Assisi, entitled *The Sermon to the Birds*, which hangs on the wall besides my wardrobe.

THE MUSCLE OF ENLIGHTENMENT

The three Abrahamic world religions, Judaism, Christianity and Islam, are connected by one progenitor, Abraham. Uncountable disputes, battles and wars have arisen among his innumerable descendants since Abraham was called by God to leave the house of his father and settle in the land of Canaan, promised by God to Abraham and his progeny. Abraham would surely turn in his grave could he see the pain and suffering that his decision set in motion over the centuries. What have I done? Or would he exclaim: What hast Thou done?

I view these three world religions as stacked on top of each other, each subsequent a reaction to the previous one: Christianity a response to Judaism, and Islam a response to Christianity. Christianity provided the Messiah promised by Judaism, and Islam provided the Last Prophet following Christianity's Jesus. Where Judaism deals with the issue of power, there Christianity focusses on sacrifice and Islam concentrates on obedience. All three are valuable aspects of an overall world view and way of living. This paragraph contains enough controversy to wage another war.

In the same way, I see Buddhism as a reaction to Hinduism. The Buddha lived around 500 BCE, in a time when

Hinduism, in his view, was focussing on too many Gods, formal precepts and traditions void of meaning. The Buddha reacted to the passivity and laziness of the Hindu faith in his time and felt that it is attachment rather than God, actions in past lives, fate, type of birth or efforts in this life that is causing our experience of suffering. His Buddhism centres on mastering non-attachment.

The essence of Hinduism is fearlessness. The great epics Ramayana and Mahabharata (which includes the Hindu classic Bhagavad Gita) recount the heroic deeds of princesses and princes, kings and queens, who courageously went into battle, not afraid to lose their lives as an honourable death would better unburden their karma and coming incarnations. Yet, around 500 BCE, the world was in need of more intelligent, subtle and focussed ways of attention. The Buddha lived around the same time as Kong Fu Tzu (Confucius) in China and Socrates in Greece.

Taoism in China goes back thousands of years. According to Chinese sources, the original version of the I Ching (The Book of Changes) was composed by Fu Hsi around 2000 BCE. Around 500 BCE, Kong Fu Tzu added commentaries, known as the Ten Wings (I Ching III). Around the same time, Lao Tzu wrote the evergreen Tao Te Ching (the power of the path) and Sun Tzu his acclaimed Bing Fa, popularised in the West as *The Art of War*. Where Taoism concentrates on balance, Confucianism concentrates on discipline.

My practice of Buddhism started out with a retreat in the north of Thailand. Together with a friend, I enjoyed a course with extensive lecturing, meditation practices and outings to various sanctuaries. The leader of Buddhism in northern Thailand, the Venerable Pradhamasathit, granted us an audition twice. The first time was at a formal meeting or ritual where we participated in greeting (with joined palms), bowing (while smiling) and prostrating (fully, flat to the ground). The second time we savoured a personal talk, with the help of an interpreter.

My second experience was the three-month Winter (or Rainy Season) Retreat in Plum Village, France, led by the late Thich Nhat Hanh, a Vietnamese Thien (or Zen) Buddhist. Apart from the teachings by Thay (Master), we were educated in small groups by other monks and we had our daily chores. I couldn't see or feel much difference between the Theravada tradition of Thailand and the Mahayana tradition of Thien Buddhism. This is probably caused by the fact that these two major traditions of Buddhism met and mingled in Vietnam.

In both retreats I experienced a blend of Buddha reverence, ancestor veneration and worship of all kinds of deities. Although Buddhism doesn't acknowledge a creating deity (Brahma in Hinduism), I experienced the whole atmosphere, with the rituals, the imagery and the precepts for worship, as purely religious. The *Sutras* that were read sometimes referred to the Absolute or a hierarchy of higher beings. There is undoubtedly a distinguishing difference from the Abrahamic religions with Buddhism's emphasis on self-experience, self-examination and self-determining, in asking, what is it like for you?

In my view, you cannot separate Buddhism from its regional, cultural and religious embedding. The spirits, the devas, the worship, the ancestors, they are all part of the totality of the practice. The intent is non-attachment, not detachment. The variation of meditations, rituals, teachings, eating habits and noble silence makes up the totality and within and through this variation, spiritual advancement towards enlightenment is made. Many atheists and former Christians turn to Buddhism to be finally freed of God. But God is just a concept, an idea, an attachment.

The Buddha promotes direct experience and calls formal and abstract religious concepts vain, empty and laughable. Only when there is a real experience, it becomes possible to explore this experience and, if it contains any suffering, to let the Four Noble Truths do their wholesome work. In summary form: suffering exists; it has a cause; it has an end and there is a way to its end. But first we need to get out of our minds and into our experience. The Buddha doesn't want us to blame God.

The Buddha is not an atheist but rather a sceptic who is against religious speculations, including speculations about a creator god. He doesn't want us to focus on a creating deity. As a reasonable alternative he comes up with 'the doctrine of dependent origination' whereby all phenomena arise in dependence on other phenomena, hence no primal unmoved mover can be acknowledged or discerned. When there's no beginning, there's no beginning act, and this is the core of the teaching. Because the act of creating sets the wheel in motion.

He wants us to focus on the present and what is present in our minds now. He wants us to examine and see through the illusions in our minds. He wants us to free our minds. The history and diversity of Buddhism are full of gods: different gods, ghosts, evil ones, good ones, big and small. There is no need to cut them off and destroy them. Through completely realising our fullness of illusions, we are heading towards a deeper emptiness. By acknowledging all, we draw near the void.

Secular Buddhism is a strange concept. We come to the Buddha, our new God, and we say: 'All's well, but I wish to hold on to one illusion. Let me make this clear from the start. No God, okay? And to prevent this from becoming a problem later on, I would like to rule this possibility out now. No religion, okay?' If you start with one skeleton in the closet - hidden, invisible, banned - and so fraught with emotion, how can you expect to become free, unattached, peaceful?

The funny thing is that Buddhism can have an enlightening effect on your faith, if you have one. You learn to look at your personal religious convictions from the viewpoint of attachment and suffering. You undertake a review and an assessment of your belief in God. Or your belief in no God. You find out, more honestly and more accurately, what is true for you and what is not. You understand, on a deeper level, what religion is really about and you remove all false, imposed and aggravating beliefs.

The Awakened One calls you to awaken. This is a continuous process, not a straight road with a white house on the horizon. Enlightenment is a constant unfolding of self; you never know what's next. 'Working on enlightenment is like training a muscle', Thich Nhat Hanh said. 'That counts for me as well', he added. 'If you don't train, the muscle becomes weak again'. I was so happy with this insight. It made so much sense. The Work appeared so simple. No brilliant, unattainable goals. Just the daily stuff.

For me, the beauty of Buddhism is its innate hopefulness. You can always start again. You can start now. I may see The Awakened One today or I may not. I may meet the Absolute today or I may not. Being mindful in my next step, in my next move, in my next breath, is all I have to care about. Looking with the eye of kindness and compassion to my inner turmoil, nourishes my inner peace. The invitation is always there. Playfully, I am becoming a merciful master.

WITH A THROW OF COINS

In the early 1990s, an intern at my work gave me a little book as a present, *The Pocket I Ching* (1988). I have never seen her again and I don't even remember her name but she's had a huge influence on my life. Having a wide interest in the wisdom of the Orient, I already knew about this Chinese classic. Reading C.G. Jung, I was familiar with the concepts of meaningful coincidence and synchronicity. But I was also sceptical and reserved about the use of new age oracles.

Yet, this was a friendly and inviting booklet, nothing like the thick tome by the same author, Richard Wilhelm, which, by the way, contains an introduction by Jung. With my Protestant background, I felt I was relinquishing myself to the Devil as I opened the book and followed the instructions to arrive at a certain chapter. There are 64 chapters with both Chinese and English titles and each chapter carries a Chinese sign. With a few throws of three random coins, one is supposed to pick a particular chapter.

The basic entity of the I Ching is the hexagram (from Greek *hexa*, meaning six), a figure composed of six stacked horizontal lines. Each line is either broken or unbroken. The I Ching contains all 64 possible hexagrams. The idea is that you enter the I Ching with a certain issue or problem that's on your mind. Concentrating on your question, you then throw the three coins six times while noting the outcomes in heads and tails. Heads count for 3 and tails count for 2. Add them up.

Now you have six throws of either 6, 7, 8 or 9. Even is *yin* and a broken line: - -. Uneven is *yang* and an unbroken line: ---. Your first throw sets the bottom line of the hexagram, your second throw the next line up, and so on and so forth. Now, look up your specific hexagram on a chart and read what the I Ching has to say about your chosen issue. This is the moment of truth, delivered to you by way of meaningful coincidence.

According to common Western rational thinking, this whole procedure is nonsense of course. It is pure coincidence that you arrive at a certain chapter and it's only your own mind and interpretation that can give you an insight. Another chapter would have given another answer to your question, probably just as wise and applicable. The orthodox Christian would add that this indeed is a questionable course of action. Leave divination to the divine, don't seek solace in black magic with coins and cards and pray to the Lord instead.

Some people prefer reading the I Ching throughout or just pick a chapter by title, out of interest. It's an ancient, oriental book of wisdom and it can teach you a lot this way too. I prefer the method using the coins. With important questions and far-reaching decisions, I consult the I Ching in the way described above. To inspire me, not to blindly follow its lead. Which is quite hard if not impossible because the language of the I Ching isn't specific. It leaves ample room for interpretation.

Say, for instance, that your issue is whether or not to find a new job. Up comes No 37 Tjia - The Clan. The text speaks of support, saying that a family that thrives is one in which good contact is cultivated. Real strength works inside out. Reading this, you realise that your current basis in life is probably not strong enough for a next step up and that you might better work on improving the bonding with your spouse and children. You realise now, you wanted to escape.

To me, consulting the I Ching is like talking to a wise friend or mentor. A conversation begins in my head and continues for the next hour, comes back the next day and when I read the guidance in question again after a week or a month, I tend to see different points of view, have other intuitions and come to better courses of action. It's always me that decides what to do and I am using other information, conversations and impressions too. The I Ching is a teacher.

About synchronicity. Apart from being a marvellous music album by Sting and The Police, it is a concept popularised by Jung. He defined synchronicity as 'the meaningful coincidence of two or more events where something other than the probability of chance is involved'. Things happen at the same time, there's no logical or causal connection and yet it seems to have meaning. Consulting the I Ching with a few throws of coins assumes such a connection. A mysterious force connects my inner motives with the way the coins fall.

I personally assume that a collective field of consciousness exists that goes beyond the individual consciousness but can be tapped into by the well-attuned. This is similar to what psychiatrist Albrecht Mahr has named 'the knowing field' (Mahr, 1999) and biologist Rupert Sheldrake has called 'morphic resonance' (Sheldrake, 1988). 'There is a deeper wave than this', musician Sting states (1985). However it works, I experience an intuitive affinity with and an intelligent meaning from the hexagrams that emerge after tossing the coins, while holding a specific issue in mind.

We have now entered the world of Taoism, a religion and a philosophy. Today, the Taoist religion is the main religion of the Republic of China (Taiwan) and it is one of the religious doctrines officially recognised by the People's

Republic of China, besides, among others, Buddhism and Confucianism. Taoism, in the core, is about balance, balancing the *yin* and *yang* forces, in all areas. I view Confucianism (from Kong Fu Tzu, who lived around 500 BCE) as a refinement of ancient Taoism, but many Confucianists and Taoists disagree.

Taoism cherishes the Tao, which is sometimes translated as 'the way'. It's hard to describe it in one English word. The Tao is generally defined as the source of everything and the ultimate principle underlying reality. Taoism emphasises living in harmony with the Tao and it promotes *wu wei* (action without intention), naturalness, simplicity, spontaneity and the Three Treasures: compassion, soberness and humility. When one follows the Tao, things go well and smoothly. The popular 'being in the flow' could be a Taoist expression. Balancing the Tao feels natural.

In society, in our relationships, in ourselves, different states occur that are constantly changing, following more or less fixed patterns. If one can see the pattern between these states, one can intuitively sense towards what state the current state is developing. What is small will become bigger. What is full will become empty. What is low will rise. In addition, deviations of balance do occur, expressed by the term 'too'. 'Too' is always too much, too little, too fast, too slow, too high, too low, and this will change.

The Tao Te Ching (Lao Tzu, 500 BCE) is another Taoist masterpiece. Long ago, a friend left this book with his things while he went traveling. Each time I stored a postal for him, I saw the book and read some. Too strange. Years later I found the same edition on the internet. I bought it, read it and still its meaning mostly evaded me. This made me furious and it made me laugh. The book seemed like an untamed horse. I tucked it far away in my bookcase.

Last year, suddenly, I had an inclination. Let's try again! I'd just read Sun Tzu's classic, *The Art of War*, and, with a heavy heart, I set myself to Lao Tzu again. Now, 58 years of age, I grasped some of its meaning. Not all of it, not by a long way, and certainly not comprehensively, yet I felt its wisdom resonate with me. Is it age? Is it growth? Is it experience? Is it readiness? I don't know. I don't feel wiser. But before I wasn't stupid either!

Next on my travel list is a trip to Taiwan, to a Taoist school. I always wished to go to a Japanese monastery with a view of Mount Fuji, but it seems it is all Zen monasteries there. Taiwan has the best Taoist schools, or so I've heard. I fear this might come out the same as reading the Tao Te Ching before. I may search for years! Somehow, someone or something is playing a trick on me. Maybe, secretly, this actually is the teaching, coming from far beyond.

THREE WISE MEN

Last night I dreamt that I came to a foreign village and that I was laid on a bed for a welcoming ceremony. As I thought my friends had organised this, I agreed, though not whole-heartedly. As I was lying there, an Indian procession approached my feet and a figure with the head of an elephant leant over me and touched my chin with his trunk. All in solemn ritualistic movements. After the ceremony, I found out, none of my friends had anything to do with the whole thing.

Waking up, I looked up the function of the Hindu God Ganesh, for it is he who is usually depicted with the head of an elephant. Wikipedia graciously informed me: 'He is widely revered, more specifically, as the remover of obstacles and thought to bring good luck; the patron of arts and sciences; and the deva of intellect and wisdom. As the god of beginnings, he is honoured at the start of rites and ceremonies. Ganesh is also invoked as a patron of letters and learning during writing sessions.'

You will understand that, especially at the last sentence, I was bewildered. As I am approximately halfway through writing this book, I feel I am being blessed by the Indian deity Ganesh. His other traits also fit well with composing

40

a spiritual book dedicated to The Beyond. More than thirty years ago I watched on TV, for the first time, a three-hour performance of the Hindu epic Mahabharata. This ancient epos is narrated by the sage Vyasa and transcribed instantly, without pause, by his aide, yes, the God Ganesh.

The Mahabharata has been a huge source of inspiration to me over the last decades, as readers of my earlier books can tell. I know excerpts by heart. It has been some years since I watched Peter Brook's movie (1989) and I had to look up the part of Ganesh in the story, just now. I hadn't planned to write this chapter about Hinduism today, but it feels appropriate now. I bow in reverence to Lord Ganesh. Next year, it will be thirty years since I first visited India.

On arrival in Delhi, I travelled to the north, to an ashram in the foothills of the Himalayas. *Haidakhan Vishwa Mahadham*, a sanctity constructed by and dedicated to Shri Babaji, is located on the bank of the river Gautami Ganga. Babaji was popularised by the pop group Supertramp in a song of the same name. I stayed and worked in this ashram over Christmas. Tradition has it that the Western guests at the ashram perform a Christmas play before some eight hundred local Indians who also receive free food.

I was chosen to perform the role of one of the Magi, the one who's traditionally known as Melchior, the oldest of the Three Wise Men. We even had a genuine director for a day, we rehearsed and, at the actual performance on Christmas Day, at the *moment supreme*, in front of this large, turbulent crowd, I felt I should expand my stage presence by adding a spoken line: 'I bring Thee gold!'. My first stage role ever, at the age of six, was also one of the Magi.

Besides such frivolous festivities, I was seriously meditating during ritual bathing, collective chanting and community cooking. I met some very weird, lovely people, was astonished by the dedication to a spiritual master already dead for ten years and had a few deep and lasting spiritual experiences myself. Looking back, I believe it was an initiation although I cannot say into what. I celebrated my 31st birthday in the ashram as well. The most important aspect was, perhaps, my sobriety as I had turned into an alcoholic, back in Amsterdam.

Of all the hundreds of Hindu Gods and the 108 sacred Names of God, I have personally always felt most attracted to Lord Shiva, the destroyer of ignorance. Shiva is part of the Trimurti, the trinity of supreme divinity in Hinduism, with Brahma as the creator, Shiva as the destroyer and Vishnu as the preserver. I have always sensed a keen resemblance with the Christian doctrine of the Trinity, which consists of the Father (creator), the Son (Jesus Christ, the transformer) and the Holy Spirit (the power to endure).

Mata Amritanandamayi, a world-famous hugging guru from Kerela, India, has made various lengthy world tours past gymnasia and public auditoria, giving a loving hug to thousands of people each day. I have been at such meetings a few times and have felt overwhelmed by the atmosphere of warmth, love and kindness in the space. I haven't found anything of similar power anywhere in the world. The energy present has a density that is almost palpable. The memory of being there reminds me that experiencing merging love is actually possible.

I visited one of her ashrams in Kerela when I happened to be nearby for Ayurvedic treatment, but she wasn't there at the time and the feeling was totally different. I resided at the Pranavam clinic of Dr Sreejith for three month-long Pancha Karma retreats over the course of two years. Pancha Karma is an ancient and sophisticated Hindu cleansing cure, including daily massage, special nutrition and herbal medicine. The thorough treatment gradually relieved the chronical headache I had had for over a year and made it more manageable.

I learned much about the body and the mind and their connection too. I caught myself having dumb prejudices about the quality of traditional Indian medicine as compared to contemporary Western medicine. What does such a country doctor treating a bunch of natives really know, I secretly though at first. But I became more and more impressed by the scientific comprehension and precision of Ayurvedic medicine. It is a vast, complete and thorough body of knowledge about the human organism, physically, mentally and spiritually, often surpassing its Western counterpart.

I may be stepping on sensitive toes asserting that I haven't noticed much difference between meditation taught by Hindu or by Buddhist practitioners. In Hindu tradition, nirvana (or *moksha*) is the reuniting with the universal God or universal soul. A soul reaches this state after living many lifetimes while climbing up through the caste system. The Buddha taught that anyone might achieve higher enlightenment and escape from the cycle of death and rebirth if they followed the right path. This completely rejected the Hindu caste structure of his time.

In 2023 I celebrate my fortieth year as a meditator and it all started in 1983 in my college town Groningen, in the north of Holland. I joined a yoga class, presented by Koos Zondervan, in the Kashmir tradition that was introduced in the West by Mr Jean Klein in the fifties. This approach concentrates on bodily positions and movements, breathing exercises and silent or guided meditation. Though I still practise the physical exercises now and then, I have mainly focussed on developing my own style of silent meditation.

I still believe that the breath is the best, simplest and deepest focus for meditation, yet for me personally it's the hard way. Although I often say how important it is to follow the breath and to practise yoga breathing exercises, the truth is that I barely do it myself. I immediately plead guilty on the charge of laziness, yet it just isn't really my thing. I do have a discipline of sitting in silence one or two times a day for twenty minutes and I'm proud of it!

Through the years, I have witnessed the growth and acceptance of yoga in modern society. When I started, one was considered to be either a socks and sandals type or a new age freak. Today, business leaders promote yoga as a human resources tool. There are yoga schools all around and also within many fitness centres. Some of these classes seem in name contradictory to the spirit of yoga, like power yoga or quick-fit yoga, but who am I to judge as I have never joined these courses myself!

I am contented that so many people in the West have found yoga and meditation as tools for relaxation, health and spiritual development. A traditional yoga teacher once asserted that relaxation is only a by-product of meditation. The genuine aim is understanding the relationship between body and mind. The longer you accustom yourself to the regularity of a meditation practice, the deeper you sink into a distinguishing awareness within your consciousness. This is your best ally against the attacks from your ego or superego on your way towards bliss.

THE SPACE IS YOURS

I've said some things about Islam in a previous chapter when I declared my love for Rumi. I spoke about Sufism, Islam's most spiritual branch, a movement that principally underlines the unity of all religions and wherein man and woman are considered equal. The other two branches of Islam are more monotheistic and the position of women is, to Western standards, a concern. Over the last two decades, Islam has gotten a bad rep in the West, starting with the 9/11 attacks, yet the feud has more ancient roots.

The fearful image of the Arab with the scimitar is deeply ingrained in Western culture. This goes back to the Fall of Constantinople in 1453, a Western defeat that marked the end of the Roman Empire. Maybe an even earlier date can be established when we consider the Crusades, following the Council of Clermont in 1095 led by Pope Urban II who called up a war against the invasions in the Holy Land by the 'Turks and Arabs' 'to destroy this vile race from the lands of our friends'.

The Abrahamic lineage has a thing with second sons. The Bible recounts that first Abraham fathers a son with his slave Hagar, Ishmael, and then a second son with his wife Sarah, Isaac. On God's instigation, Abraham sends

Hagar and Ishmael away and his second son Isaac inherits all. With Esau and Jacob, Isaac's sons, second son Jacob deceives their blinded father to receive Esau's birth right. Jacob fathers two sons with his first chosen wife Rachel and the eldest, Joseph, is sold as a slave by his brothers.

Ishmael is generally considered to be the ancestor of the Ishmaelites or Northern Arabs. In the narrative in the Quran, he is the son of the near-sacrifice, not Isaac (who is not yet born). It is Ishmael who stands alongside Abraham in their attempt to set up the Kaaba in Mecca as a place of monotheistic pilgrimage. And Ishmael is the distant ancestor of Muhammad, the Prophet. So the Quran just skips the whole second son thing and leaves it to the Jews (and Christians) to fight it out.

Muhammad founded Islam in the seventh century and is called The Last Prophet. He was illiterate and when he was instructed to pass along the Holy Quran, he ordered a few dozen scribes to transcribe his teaching. This way, any individual mistakes could later be rectified by comparing transcriptions. The Pali Canon, the oldest surviving text of Buddhism, was recorded 500 years after the Buddha had passed away. The Gospels in the Bible were probably written 40-60 years after Jesus' life. I imagine, Muhammad had learned from his colleagues.

Obedience, purification and refinement are, in my view, the essential elements of Islam. Obedience sounds better than submission, but it implies the same loyalty. It simply is obedience to Allah, in the same manner that Saint Francis chose obedience to God as the first of his three vows. Western people, and particularly the Dutch, often have a problem with obedience because they think this threatens their autonomy, individuality or freedom. Luther's famous quote 'Here I stand; I can do no other' expresses the same intention to listen to God.

Exchange 'god' for 'good' and no one has a problem with that. Nearly everybody wishes to be good and to do good. And, as we are all personally responsible people, we all answer to our own conscience (and, of course, to the law). Whatever goes between God or Allah and me is my business. There's no essential difference between a person who only answers to God and a person who only answers to their own conscience. For it is you who mingles between the two or who chooses one.

Obedience in Islam is expressed when the *muezzin* proclaims the *adhan* for the daily prayer from the *minaret* at the mosque five times a day. Obedience is expressed when the believers, together in the mosque or individually on their prayer mat, bow and kneel down to the ground, following a set order. Obedience is expressed when the faithful respect the precepts of their faith and hold back from bad deeds. Obedience is expressed when Muslims refrain from food, drink and sex in the daytime during the month called Ramadan.

Purification shows itself in the ritual of *wudu*, the washing of face, hands, arms and feet before praying. This has a deep symbolic meaning. It expresses the desire to cleanse the soul from impurity and the wish to appear before Allah unstained. *Wudu* expresses the same wish as the absolution of sins in the Catholic sacrament. In Amsterdam, I joined a local shopkeeper a few times to the Friday afternoon prayer at his mosque nearby. Looks and gestures made me feel truly welcome and soon I naturally merged in.

Purification in Islam is also fostered by praying, reciting and sharing. By giving alms, attention and advice to people around who are in need, the heart is purified of selfishness. The aim of the religious activity called *azkiyah* is directed to 'sanctification' or 'purification' of the self. This refers to the process of transforming the primitive, crude *nafs* (ego-desires or man's unrefined nature) from their deplorable state of self-centrality through various spiritual stages towards a level of purity and submission, resulting in a fully aligned spiritual awareness of Allah.

In this refinement, personal, spiritual and religious development come together. Personal Higher Will is the key insight that the only thing I really want, deep down inside, is to be aligned to Universal Will. This doesn't involve a limitation of my freedom. It means experiencing my total freedom as an individual to follow my own deepest inner motives, values and heart desires. It is only when I, deliberately or not, out of ignorance or pain, deviate from what is good and kind that I, and those around me, suffer.

Refinement can also be perceived in Islamic calligraphy. Pictures have traditionally been limited in Islamic books in order to avoid idolatry. Instead, there is a long history in calligraphy and handwriting which is strongly tied to the Quran. Chapters and excerpts from the Quran are commonly the texts upon which Islamic calligraphy is based. An ancient Arabic proverb illustrates the wholesomeness of refinement suggesting that 'purity of writing is purity of the soul'. The Prophet Muhammad is related to have said: 'The first thing God created was the pen'.

That's always nice to hear for a writer! I have this experience of refinement by writing too, even without the craft of calligraphy. My head becomes clearer, my heart becomes softer, my soul becomes more knowledgeable. This doesn't mean that I don't have to practise and perfect the valuable outcomes in real life. I do, I try, I progress, I fail, I learn. When I return to the writing table, I can sense how these daily wins and losses are working inside me as a kind of spiritual digestion.

I need to have and, more important, take the time and the space to let this process evolve, maturate and crystallise. When I give it up in favour of all the everyday trivialities that seem important but really are not, I end up hating myself, blaming others and in need of more dulling trivia. The most important gift I need, can give myself and ask from my intimates, is the gift of allowing inner concentration. The Work that goes on inside isn't usually pretty or easy but yields gold.

This inner space is, in my experience, symbolised in the architecture and design of the mosque. Other sanctuaries

are usually full of stuff: pews and chairs, statues and paintings, candlesticks and flowerpots, frills and folderols and
an altar or a pulpit. A mosque is an open space with a de-
cent rug. Admittedly, a mosque commonly holds a *minbar*,
a pulpit on which the imam stands to deliver the sermon.
Yet, this piece of furniture is mostly small compared to the
space that is free for sitting, kneeling and praying.

One of the most spacious, transcendent and spiritual
mosques I have ever visited, is the Sabanci Central Mosque
in Adana, the second largest mosque in Turkey and named
after one of its wealthiest families. It can host up to 28,500
believers. The open space, yet perfectly contained, seemed
like the ultimate reminder and mirror of what could be my
inner space, inviting me to explore my own spiritual and
religious realm. The open nature of the building and the
effect of the architecture bore into me a deep peace.

THERE'S A PLACE FOR US

The age of 42 is sometimes called midlife and a midlife crisis sometimes accompanies this landmark year. I spent most of my 42nd year of life in a rehab centre, dealing with a drinking problem. Already into spirituality, I preferred a place with a spiritual approach, Arta, an anthroposophical institute, working from the philosophy of Rudolf Steiner, the German (educational) philosopher. Anthroposophy is mainly known by the Waldorf or Steiner education whose schools are found in Germany (*die Freie Schule*), Holland (*de Vrije School*), the UK and the US.

In the Netherlands, anthroposophy is also the basis of a holistic academy and a licensed health institute. Addiction care is organised as a separate department within its psychiatric clinic. I'd had some disappointing experiences in regular addiction care that concentrates on cognitive and behavioural therapy. A psychiatrist friend of mine referred me to Arta, a holistic institute, that offered in-patient care. To start, I had to agree to be admitted to a closed ward for at least two months which involved staying at a rural farm-house hosting twelve patients.

No substances, no visitors, no interim departures, no return policy. It was a real pressure cooker, with characters from all walks of life (although the rich and famous have their private institutes, of course!). Participants were required to fully detox which implied *cold turkey* for the lovers of heroin, cocaine and crack. For us, alcoholics, it was easy, for the body is detoxified in 24 hours. For hard drug users, it can take 3 to 6 months. Especially at night, it was a real circus, yet I stood tall.

As there was a lot of room for expression and creativity in the program, I immediately dived behind the piano. I played at home too, but here I went all out. I composed songs, set mystical poems to music and was encouraged to perform before the group. Not everyone liked my musical works of course, but the leadership endorsed my way of artistic detoxification. The soul is a concept and an entity that is welcomed in anthroposophy. In fact, anthroposophy can be seen as the science of the soul.

In a playful way, I became free from alcohol and discovered my deeper talents, wishes and aspirations. Apart from the creative possibilities (also drawing, painting and moulding lessons were offered), there was special attention for body movement (eurhythmics), nature experience and daily work in kitchen, garden and household. There were group sharings and personal therapy sessions. There were outings and farewell parties. I had a lovely time with my fellow 'inmates', as we mockingly called each other. Altogether, I was away from home and work for a full year.

Anthroposophy has a religious branch too, but we were not bothered with that. The Christian Community (German: *Die Christengemeinschaft*) is a Christian denomination. This is more of an adjacent area. Anthroposophy comes from the word *'anthropos'*, Greek for 'human '. This holistic and integral approach is directed at developing the human potential, creatively, mentally and spiritually. It's not religious in nature. And I could sense that during my year off in this wonderful, warm and wise home. According to my purified consciousness something was missing, on a subtle level.

Something in my soul was not mirrored in this institute and program. Of course, there were individual talks and expressions of a personal nature during that year showing a religious interest or awareness, but it was not formally or energetically part of the package. I was so busy, comfy and happy with all possibilities that were offered that I did not pay much attention to this at the time. Later on, however, I saw it, thought about it and seemed to understand this spiritual lack. God was not acknowledged.

When I say 'God' here, I am not specifically referring to the Christian or Abrahamic belief in a supreme being. In my view, it can point to any god or gods or deity or supernatural, mystical or universal being. I am indicating a general religious dimension as to be distinguished from a general spiritual dimension. If you have no sense of, feeling for, intuition about or experience with what I am saying, this may be hard to understand. I do believe everyone has the potential to develop this awareness.

The energetic experience of missing a religious element in an otherwise fine spiritual setting is of course hard to describe (for me) and hard to grasp (for you) if one doesn't have such an impression or awareness oneself. In the spiritual dimension, I experience connection, love, gentleness, frictions, joy, compassion, peacefulness and pure and momentarily manifesting emotions as fear, anger and sadness. I sense and perceive this field energetically at the level of the belly and heart of the people (or group of people) present in a certain circumstance.

In the religious dimension, I sense the same as in the spiritual dimension plus an extra energetical layer over or behind it as it were, a subtle field that encloses, encompasses or surrounds the spiritual realm. In addition, there is a subtle energetic presence at the height of the heads of the people (or group of people) who are there. The field is wider, denser and higher. This religious field feels deeper, lighter and gentler. It is impersonal, objective and refined. This gives the impression of sacred, holy, stilled.

This is just my perception. I am not describing an absolute truth. I am not saying that the people who 'only' perceive the spiritual dimension are dumber, thicker or less advanced. I am not implying that I have a direct line with God him or herself. I am also not dismissing anthroposophy or the former Arta community. I am deeply grateful for the opportunity I had to stay and learn there. In a way, it saved my life. The group and the staff, from that time, inspire me still.

Different places have different strengths and weaknesses. In the end, we are all human, fallible, learning, growing. In the Benedictine monasteries where I stayed over the last seven years, I felt the religious field to be stronger than the spiritual field, as the spiritual is a more human, relating and connecting operative. This is perfectly logical and absolutely not a fault of the monasteries or the monks. Their tantric skills have also not convinced me until now, but maybe I haven't yet been able to look behind the curtain!

Missing something in an otherwise great setting is just the drive of perfection that is starting to work. A certain level of perfection extends the invitation for a still higher level of perfection. Perfection challenges, tickles, stimulates. The fire of perfection is not aroused by a mundane or ordinary experience of reality. Only that which is already adequate, agreeable and admirable awakens the desire for a supreme wholeness. The horse smells the barn and deploys its last ounce of strength to rush towards the awaited bliss of the stable.

It is the transformation from mud to lotus, as the Venerable Thich Nhat Hanh called it. Without mud, no lotus. Suffering from addiction - and I am not referring to myself in particular - bears an enormous hurt and a great sadness. This is mud, for sure. Having been given the opportunity to do something about it and to experience the rise after such a deep fall, is humbling, satisfying and encouraging. When I came home after the whole thing had been completed and accomplished, I felt truly blessed.

Arta had a success rate of 50 percent which is considered very high in the world of addiction care. Regular addiction care has to settle for 30 percent. I made it through and without relapse. This is 18 years ago. Sure, this is my own achievement. The day I started anew, the (symbolic) second half of my life, I felt I was walking the tightrope. I could easily slip and fall. That I didn't was not just because of my own power or the quality of the Arta program.

It was mostly through bowing. Not considering myself grand. Proceeding with caution, knowing that temptation is just around the corner. Avoiding greatness and counteracting weakness. Embracing the pain of life. Realising that everybody hurts, sometimes. Taking comfort in a friend. Holding on. I felt that grace had been bestowed upon me. I had surrendered to forces greater than me. It wasn't just luck and it wasn't just my merit. There are powers far beyond our understanding. I bowed to the Great Spirit, to the mountain and to the winds.

THE ART OF SURRENDER

Somewhere in my late twenties, I was on holiday with my then-girlfriend. We had been together for about two years. I had just finished my studies at university and was doing some projects as a freelance management consultant. Having sort of left my university town, I was on the move, living here and there, staying with friends, a phase of wandering, probably leading towards a more stable situation. On holiday in France by car, we stopped at a super-cosy inn with good food and a simple yet comfy room.

We had this habit of reading to each other. We sometimes picked up a book one of us was devouring and read some appealing passage aloud to each other. This time one of us - I don't remember who - had brought a copy of *Zen and the Art of Motorcycle Maintenance* by Robert M. Pirsig, a book from 1974. It is a fictionalised autobiography of a 17-day journey that Pirsig made on his Honda CB77 motorcycle from Minnesota to Northern California along with his son Chris in 1968.

In this narrative, Pirsig explores his concept of Quality. The Zen-aspect is reflected in the mindfulness in actions - in this case motorcycle maintenance - and, by continued, careful concentration, to become perfectly at one with the action. The nature of mystical experience plays an underlying role in the book. It is, above all, very entertaining. We felt amused, inspired, loving towards each other, really in the moment, gradually forgetting the outside world entirely. The atmosphere between us condensed, the light softened and slowly we were becoming completely one.

I have thought of this moment a lot, later in life. If I try my best, I can still feel the density in that room, the loving atmosphere, the feeling of grace, fortune and relaxation. Normally, I'm always a bit tense, not relaxed. I can't surrender well, to love, to the situation, to the moment. I have to be caught off-guard, in a gentle way, to lose control, to let go of my idea of directing the circumstances. We could now investigate my childhood, but we take another route.

In any process of personal development, there comes a moment when you cannot do it by yourself anymore. For the next step, the next move, you need help from someone else. You have only two hands and all at once you need a third. You look around you and ask the nearest bystander to lend you a hand. Or you are working on a personal issue about leadership and it suddenly dawns upon you that you cannot fix this yourself. You need the input, the feedback from a friend.

At the intersection of personal development and spiritual development, this starts happening more often and on a deeper level. The message being sent is that you need others in order to grow. Simple but true. At this stage you need to surrender to someone or something else, it can be a person, nature, the universe or a higher being. In the act of reaching out, of connecting, of asking, and then, in the instant of receiving, accepting and absorbing what is given, you momentarily lose your mind, your ego.

Normally, we don't pay much attention to this interchange. We say 'thanks' a million times a day, give a friendly glance and move on. When we are in trouble, it becomes a different story. We will always remember the friend or relative who was there for us in our hour of need. Often, accepting help is accompanied by a feeling of shame, of failure, not being able to manage on our own. The art of receiving help, attention, support, appreciation, acknowledgement and love is much underrated. And so needed.

Another moment when I felt completely at ease with myself in the situation I was in, happened in Plum Village, the mindfulness centre in France. I had just performed a self-composed song in front of an audience sitting patiently on the floor. It was Christmas Eve and open-mic night; a range of lovely and personal performances, singing, reciting, jamming. When I had finished my song, moving from dead-nervous to joyfully relieved, I sat among the super-relaxed audience and felt myself miraculously merging with the community, the atmosphere, my surroundings.

If you do something that is out of the ordinary, something that expands your boundaries, something you have wanted all your life but were too afraid to pursue, you can have this experience of leaving your old, narrow self behind, very briefly. Suddenly you feel totally fresh, totally open, totally new, stripped of all the common daily ballast that is normally holding and wearing you down. It is the thrill and motive of mountaineers, deep-sea divers, artists in general and the spiritually brave. You feel absolutely and utterly alive.

Traveling through the US for three months, I came to Flagstaff, Arizona, one day. The following morning, early at dawn, I took the first bus to Kaibab National Forest and arrived in thick fog. I hiked the designated trail to the start of the descent, wondering if it would be safe to continue my journey. Then the fog started to clear and, all of a sudden, I looked into the majestic depth of the Grand Canyon and over to the North Rim. I was blown away, full of awe.

As it was early and because I'd taken a local bus, there was hardly anyone around. I felt the grandiosity of nature like I had never felt it before. Wow! The scale of the canyon was just too enormous to take in and the surprise in the experience added to the feeling of being inexpressibly overwhelmed. The effect on my consciousness was a sense of complete merging with my surroundings. For a minute, I lost the feeling of 'I', although this was never scary and came nowhere near psychotic.

The feeling of oneness with the whole cosmos doesn't need to be grand, loud or ecstatic. It can be very small, still and intimate. Like in the bedroom, in the church or in the sauna. In sexuality, people can have the ultimate sense of becoming one with all, not only with their partner. In silent religious worship, God may descend and touch your heart. Personally, I can find total relaxation in the sauna: 'This is my church, this is where I heal my hurts'. Words and thoughts become superfluous.

Ego is separation. We all exist separately, in our own body, in our own skin, in our own mind. That is the human condition. From separation, we begin to crawl back to unity. The grand illusion is that we can *do* this. To return to unity we need to surrender. Surrendering is not a passive state of waiting, nor is it found by letting go of ambitions, interests and responsibilities. We need to surrender to an undercurrent, a flow of life, a stream of consciousness, to an inner voice.

Taoists call this the Tao. Certain religions call it Allah, Lord, Yahweh. Indigenous cultures have many names for the nature of nature, the force behind creation, the essence of beingness. Eastern wisdom speaks of the Absolute, the Divine, the Supreme. Sufism hands us words like the Beloved, the Friend, the Innkeeper. When we are in contact with this essence, we know what to do each newly occurring moment, we feel connected to a greater, deeper and wider reality and we sense meaning in the continuous unfoldment of the world.

I felt at one with all once, meditating with a hundred people in total silence. I felt at one with all once, lying on a hard bed in an Indian village undergoing an intense cleansing treatment. I felt at one with all once, making love in a cosy attic in complete surrender to lust and pleasure. I felt at one with all once, hiking alone on the Altiplano in Chile (but this may have been caused by altitude sickness). I felt at one with all once, writing a book.

Thy Will Be Done. From the Lord's Prayer, noted in the Holy Bible, Matthew 6. According to Dante Alighieri in *The Divine Comedy* from 1320, the carnal sin of Superbia, pride or hubris, is, of the seven deadly sins, the most difficult one to overcome. Surrendering to God means to bow to God, completing the movement from standing straight, nose in the air, by bending the head, the back, the knees, down to the ground, humbling myself into a kneeled posture of humility and service. Blessed are the meek.

NICE TO SEE YOU AGAIN

In the previous years, in my previous books, I have referred to the term 'karma' now and then. Of course I knew the term before. If only in joking, I have deviously pointed at the possible past lives of friends and myself throughout this life of mine. In the West, we are familiar with the fact that Eastern religions as Hinduism and Buddhism believe in reincarnation. This idea is sometimes ridiculed, degraded or dismissed as superstitious. Over the last couple of years, I have made a turn in this.

Over recent years, I have been reading Rudolf Steiner's book series *Karmic Relationships. Esoteric Studies Vol. I-VIII*, a reflection of the final lectures by the founder of anthroposophy. Steiner died in 1925. During 1924, before his last address in September, he gave, all over Europe, over eighty lectures on the subject of karma to members of the Anthroposophical Society. These profoundly esoteric lectures examine the underlying laws of reincarnation and karma. It's such a different way of thinking that I had to read the lectures over and over again.

I only do this when something essential and personal is touched. I felt Steiner was hitting on a deep truth that is not or not constructively present in Western thought. The

Abrahamic background of the Western and Arab cultures rely on sources that assume one life on Earth per person and various forms of afterlife. Judaism does not particularly focus on life after death, but it does assume immortality of the soul, 'the World to Come' and the resurrection of the dead. Christianity and Islam focus on the afterlife.

On page 10 of my book *Life Phases in Personal Development*, I write: 'Christianity, alas, only acknowledges half of eternity. It promises eternal life (under some conditions) after we die. Hinduism also accepts eternity before birth. We all come from somewhere. The concept of reincarnation allows our soul many incarnations on this Earth as we strive towards enlightenment. Karma is the notion that a person's actions in this life will change his next life. Good actions create good karma; bad actions create bad karma.' I haven't changed my mind!

I have to add that the word 'alas' in this quote was an ironic comment in the context of that book. I have nothing against the convictions of Christianity on the matter of heaven and hell. Personally, I have gradually but irresistibly been drawn towards this idea of life before birth. Conversations on reincarnation often digress into mockery about famous dead persons. A regression therapist I once talked with told me that many clients wished, secretly or not, that they'd been someone famous or important in a past life.

In the research for this book, I even stumbled across a Dutch professional association for regression and reincarnation therapists, the NVRT. Let me make it clear, I am not so much interested in the biographical content of past lives. My interest concerns two matters. Firstly, the idea of many lives, past and to come, gives a totally different perspective on this life. Secondly, assuming reincarnation, our souls take important experiences and life issues with them through many lives. Our childhood is not the only place our issues are born.

To me, the concept of reincarnation makes much more sense. I understand how the Buddha felt that the followers of Hinduism of his time had become passive and careless, hence the reason for him wanting to shake them up. Yet, he didn't doubt the truth of reincarnation. He only asserted that the path to enlightenment could be travelled more swiftly and more efficiently. The idea that God is producing soul after soul just for one life, just for a quick peek at our dreadful earthly circumstances, seems ridiculous now.

It took me years to rethink the implications of the concept of reincarnation for my existence and for my life, or better, for this life. It took me years to let this fundamentally different insight sink in and have my emotional and spiritual body become acquainted with its feel. All along, something knowing, deep within me, waited patiently and joyfully for me to catch up, welcoming me on arrival. I'm not a true believer, I'm not a fanatic (I hope), but I'm totally comfortable with this new view now.

One of the consequences of endorsing the concept of reincarnation is that I have all the time in the world to live, to learn, to develop. The perspective is much wider. I am not in a hurry and I don't have to rush through checklists and finish a bucket list. I can handle matters much more fundamentally and take the time to concentrate, enjoy and accomplish what comes my way. There's also much less fear of death, although this will have to prove itself when I kick the bucket.

A second development that is brought on by embracing reincarnation is that my relationships change, from my side anyway. Steiner also proposes the idea that the many lives we live are mainly spent around the same souls. Our many life-lessons through the ages involve the same bunch of people we are meeting and living with in this life. But since we generally have no recollection of former lives and because we can normally only perceive the body and not the soul, we have no knowledge of this funny fact.

Steiner also elaborates on the different positions wherein we meet each other through various lives. Your mother now could have been your sister in a past life. Our boss in our previous life may return as our lover in this one. My friend may have been my father, my colleague may have been my teacher and my daughter may have been my wife. And that is only in the past. For my son now could be my brother in a next life and my enemy could be my friend.

All these different people, relationships and positions through all those different lives serve just one purpose: to help me resolve my karma. Karma is a concept originally from India as well. The idea is that we, during many lives, work through a load of unrefined desires and ego illusions. This concept is the opposite of a clean slate, the *tabula rasa* or blank page. We arrive in this life with certain questions and themes that will have to be faced and answered. Together, these constitute our karma or life-lessons.

If this all seems rather deterministic, I can tell you, it's not. For, being faced with the difficulties and hardships of life, that no world view or philosophy of life will deny, we are completely free in what to do, what to think and what to learn (if anything). It is always your personal interpretation of these life-lessons that determines your view, your actions and your perception of the results. Though everyone around you tries to influence you all the time, you are completely sovereign in your own spirit.

Even I cannot change that! Karma is created by the law of cause and effect. Through our past lives, our souls have acquired difficulties, popularly said: 'our baggage'. By doing wrong, even out of ignorance, we have soiled or defiled our slate and we have to clean up the mess we have made. Gradually we penetrate our delusions, refine our false desires and restore our innate goodness. By doing good in this life, we are turning the wheel of fortune. We are freeing ourselves from unneeded and unwanted ballast.

It's just like in a normal relationship. When you forgive your past grievances and do your best to make amends and move on, you are inviting the other person to do the same. And all gets better. The law of cause and effect works both ways. This is how you and how humanity make progress.

Humanity makes progress through you. You are the only instrument humanity has to improve the world. Clearing your karma is the best option in this life and it promises the best for the next.

And if you fall… you simply get up again. Few people won't forgive an honest and full apology. I'm sorry. This simple phrase is just as relevant as: Thank you. Life doesn't need grand gestures. Simplicity will do. You will do. Just as you are. With your issues, with your emotions, with your flaws. 'All that it takes is a good human heart', the Dalai Lama once said. By adjusting small things, in your way of life, in your way of communicating, you are becoming the person you know.

A BLESSING IN DISGUISE

Muhammad heard a voice
calling him to prayer. He asked for water
to perform ablutions. He washed his hands
and feet, and just as he reached for his boot,
an eagle snatched it away! The boot turned upsidedown
as it lifted, and a poisonous snake dropped out.

The eagle circled and brought the boot back,
saying, 'My helpless reverence for you
made this necessary. Anyone who acts
this presumptuously for a legalistic reason
should be punished!'
                                    Muhammad thanked the eagle,
and said, 'What I thought was rudeness
was really love. You took away my grief,
and I was grieved! God has shown me everything,
but at that moment I was preoccupied within myself.

Rumi (translation C. Barks)
'Joy at Sudden Disappointment'
One-handed Basket Weaving, 1991

A little further on in this poem, Rumi explains and encourages:

'The eagle carries off Muhammad's boot
and saves him from snakebite.

Don't grieve for what doesn't come.

Some things that don't happen
keep disasters from happening.'

And then this beautiful definition follows:

'Someone once asked a great sheikh
what sufism was.
                    'The feeling of joy
when sudden disappointment comes.'

Sometimes we don't recognise the signs of fortune. We are sadly so fully deluded by our egos, craving for pleasure and shunning away from pain, that we blindly follow our desires: the projected line upwards, the illusions of linear progress, professional advancement and economic growth. Then we may have forgotten what personal development is really about. To develop originally meant to unroll, to unfold, and is derived from French *développer*, unwrap, unfurl, unveil; reveal the meaning of. Think also of the opposite, an envelope: something to wrap something in.

What will be coming out of our envelop when we pursue our personal growth, *that* we don't know. We can only open the envelop and take the next item out, look at it and let ourselves be touched. A more fitting image is probably that of the snake shedding its skin. That doesn't just look nice and easy, does it? Personal growth means consciously letting go of old, now useless and unneeded things in our lives and looking deep within to what is waiting and ready to come out.

What is revealing itself when we honestly look inside is not always a pretty sight. Often not, actually, as most of us live with a lot of suppressed pain, emotion and impulses. Pain and discomfort is mostly what manifests itself first, such as when you pull a plaster from an unkempt wound. Not wanting to look, not wanting to feel, has mostly aggravated the underlying injury. When it takes too long, we are forced by our organism (physically and or psychologically) to look and feel anyway. Sometimes after years.

This all may seem very nasty, but there is a huge upside too. What is revealing itself in you is something beautiful, something wonderful, something authentically yours. Yet it is covered in dirt, mud, slime, darkness, anguish and suffering. As you uncover the hidden shining diamond below, its reflecting light starts breaking through. At first only in sparks, flashes and beams but gradually lighter and brighter, unshattered in its ability to radiate in full glory. What we are discovering, craves to be uncovered, yearns to exist in broad daylight.

This is all the usual stuff about the transition from personal development to spiritual development and a piece of cake for all readers who have fully integrated my books I to VI in their being. What we are touching on now is the working of the beyond, the transition from spiritual development to religious development. This involves an active part from a transpersonal intelligence, something that is not 'I', and it concerns something that 'I' cannot accomplish myself. In all religions a greater presence is evoked at this point.

Such evocation is sought by reciting, chanting, praying and dancing and by offerings, movements and other rituals. The older the better! An evocation is not an act with a guaranteed outcome. It cannot be enforced. An evocation is an invitation. By bowing, kneeling and prostrating, the presence and the influence of higher powers is invoked, whether this happens in a rain dance, in a church liturgy or in an ancestral ceremony. Entrenched forms of evocations like swearing, little prayers and using a talisman are excessively applied by outspoken non-believers!

As the invoked powers are vastly mightier and stronger than we humans are, the effects of our evocations may be totally unforeseen and unlooked for. They may exceed our wildest expectations! Hence, the term 'blessing in disguise'. Assuming for the moment that we have invoked the right, benevolent forces, the result may at first sight seem totally undesirable and unwanted. Realising, however, our fundamental ignorance, littleness and imperfection compared to that of the Presence we beseeched, we hush in shame and wait patiently for the miracle to reveal itself.

And that, dear readers, is already nearly too much for almost all human beings. Only the Masters, the Saints, the Bodhisattva's, the Sages, only spiritually advanced human beings are capable to surrender in some extent to the Divine, to God's Will. *In sha'Allah*, God willing, Muslims say a dozen times a day. Yet to follow God's Will, to surrender to God's Will or even to know God's Will, is often too far-fetched for simple souls like you and me. What we can do is to surrender to this realisation.

This doesn't imply that we are inferior or submissive small people. As people we are valuable, loveable and admirable. Through our spiritual practice, in whatever tradition and with whatever content, we are drawn towards the fire, we receive glimpses of truth and we come closer to the mystery. We try and we keep on trying. We grow and we keep on growing. We forgive and we ask to be forgiven. If an eagle ever snatches our boot to free it from poisonous snakes, we will laugh together with Muhammad.

> Workers rush toward some hint
> of emptiness, which they then
> start to fill. Their hope, though,
> is for emptiness, so don't think
> you must avoid it. It contains
> what you need!

BEYOND PERSONAL DEVELOPMENT

Dear soul, if you were not friends
with the vast nothing inside,
why would you always be casting your net
into it, and waiting so patiently?

This invisible ocean has given you such abundance,
but still you call it 'death',
that which provides you sustenance and work.

God has allowed some magical reversal to occur,
so that you see the scorpion pit
as an object of desire,
and all the beautiful expanse around it
as dangerous and swarming with snakes.

This is how strange your fear of death
and emptiness is, and how perverse
the attachment to what you want.

The mother and father are your attachment
to beliefs and bloodties
and desires and comforting habits.

Don't listen to them!
They seem to protect,
but they imprison.
They are your worst enemies.
They make you afraid
of living in emptiness.

Some day you'll weep tears of delight,
remembering your mistaken parents!

Rumi (translation C. Barks)
'Craftmanship and Emptiness'
One-handed Basket Weaving, 1991

BUILDING THE ARK

The Hebrew Bible recounts the story of Noah's Ark, a large, wooden ship timbered by Noah himself that hid and protected him, his family and pairs of every animal species on Earth during a mighty divine deluge that erased most of humanity. Nobody believed Noah when he warned against the coming flood. Everybody ridiculed him as he was constructing this huge, strange vessel on land, far away from a sailable river or sea. But when the rains came and the water drowned everyone, Noah's family and animals were saved.

I am telling this story by heart now. I haven't looked it up in the Bible, nor anywhere else. Maybe some details are not original and created by my rich imagination as a child. For, as a child, I was captivated by this legendary tale. I felt an outsider and a loner too, mocked and bullied because of my strange ideas and deviant behaviour. Don't worry, what follows next is not a story of how I became an omniscient fortune-teller or a self-professed prophet. I do not foresee Armageddon!

Everyone's life story is unique and everybody wants to belong to other people. Many people experience a friction between these two. They feel they have to adjust to fit in. They think they have to accommodate themselves to the wishes and judgements of others. They suspect they won't be accepted when they don't. They fear their survival will be endangered when they do not conform. During their teens, many adolescents gradually give up their personal visions and ambitions. They amalgamate into the nameless, faceless crowd. Nipped in the bud.

'We don't need no education', Pink Floyd cried out in the early eighties. Close to our graduation, we organised the so-called 'last school day' or LSD, pretty subversive for Bible belt Holland. I managed to get the janitor to play this song over the intercom of the entire school of 1400 pupils at the start of the second lesson that morning. This heralded the outset of our day of lesson-free fun-packed anarchy. Freedom. I am still joyously proud of pulling off this stunt. I'd made my mark of maladjustment!

I was smart. I co-organised the whole event, scheduled a pop podium and played there myself with my own band. Conflicting interests but who cares! The only painful thing was that, at my hour of glory, the girl I wanted to impress preferred the gym where the sports fanatics played a volleyball competition. But, as rejection is the artist's nutrition, I flourished in her absence, played my gig and today I still own a recording of that memorable concert on a forty-year-old but still running cassette tape. Touch wood.

My brother and sister had given me the Pink Floyd album *The Wall* for my seventeenth birthday in 1980. The music, the lyrics, the story, its overwhelming totality sank loud and deep into my juvenile consciousness. Two years later, I was already in college, the movie came out and it devastated me, it shook my foundation. The bohemian, the artist, the suffering Werther, man against machine, soloist crushed by the system and still the soul survives. The redemption, the catharsis, the restoration of wholeness. Yet, distinctively different from Christ's'.

The Wall presents a burned-out rock star, doped to the eyeballs, jaded by drinks and broads but above all traumatised by his childhood wound from a father lost at an early age. We see his younger years as he gradually builds a wall around his heart, loses control, snaps totally and becomes a fascist frontman. Eventually, his abandoned inner child is theatrically sentenced in a monstrous fake trial for revealing his deepest fear and the final judgement is to be exposed. Tear down the wall. Children ramble the debris.

Once a year, I watch the DVD of the movie *The Wall*, knowing very well how easy and how much brighter and sharper streaming would be. It is a ritual. Naturally, I know every song, every line, every chord. I know all characters, all scenes, all transitions. Some years, I feel I have totally failed. Failed myself, my hopes and dreams, my personal aims. I gave up. Gave in. I too subsided. Some years, I am proud. I am still here, I am still trying, I am still creating.

I am approaching sixty now and I can't say it's getting easier or harder. Pros and cons change, but the sum adds up to about the same. Consciousness is a strange thing. It's ageless. I look at myself (not in the mirror) and I see the same schoolboy I told you about. I feel his aspirations. My perspective is a little wider. I can look back longer. What goes off at the front part is added at the back. Also zero sum. I am more or less the same.

I am still building the Ark. My books and my music together shape my ark. I live in them. All artists, all writers have this feeling of immanent failure. It's never enough. The author Philip Roth and the musician Sting as well as me. My work is not (yet!) very popular, but that makes no difference at all. The appreciation always remains on the outside. The public reach is always disappointing. Nobody really understands the work completely. But this is by no means a complaint. It's just a fact.

It's a funny thing. Everybody is building their own ark and this is beyond appreciation and criticism, beyond qualitative esteem and quantitative scope. It's just a crazy adventure of doing something you feel you have to do exactly the way you feel you must do it, against all odds, against all opposition and against all outcomes. In some way, the rejection, the scorn, the ridicule, are part of it. As are the applause, the seduction, the manipulation. Without outside resistance, you would probably not be doing this job well.

And within this utterly personal and soloist adventure, you can become completely free. Not free like apart from the world, deliberately different or embittered antisocial but gently savouring your perfect independence and authenticity while being in loving connection with the world. You don't let its judgements and projections get to you. You don't take in its fame and fortune. You value the limitations that the work on the Ark entails. The Work, a precious gift, that brings you more and more to the core of existence, personally and objectively.

There comes a time when the rains start pouring, when the dikes break, when the wells are full, when the ground is saturated, when the rivers overflow, when the seas flood the land. Being inside your ark, with your loved ones and some pets, you feel that the ship is slowly lifted from the ground. It wobbles slightly. The wood squeaks and creaks. This is the moment of truth. Will the vessel be seaworthy, watertight and buoyant? All these plans. All this work. All these years. All this hope.

This is your mission. This is your assignment. This is your destiny. In the dead of night, you are called to duty. Refusal is not an option. Then you would betray your own heart. You know you will go because you know you have already committed to this task, long ago or somewhere in the future. The past is pushing you and the future is pulling you. You can say no but you will say yes. There's no doubt about it. This undertaking is timeless. You become the mission.

Time is slowing down. Everything is slowing down as you continue working at the same pace. The work continues while your movements are retarding. You watch the process gradually come to a near standstill, but there continues to be a hardly perceptible pace and progress. The work just goes on, all by itself. The present is growing and becomes bigger, wider, higher, deeper, fuller. In this expanding present, you become visible. Little by little, you fill up the present. Until you become fully present. You have become the present.

Nothing stays the same. Everything changes. You can't stay here, as you have to move on, as everything moves on again. It doesn't matter. You have become the core now. Nothing can harm you anymore. You exist beyond time and place and you know you do exist. A great peace comes over you. All acting and relating from now on will originate from this new place inside of yourself and time will be of no consequence anymore. What moves doesn't move in time. What changes doesn't change in time.

TO ALL MY ANCESTORS

Paradise lies under the feet of your mother, so goes an Islamic proverb. My local Islamic grocer told me this when we talked about the caregiving to our ageing mothers. This is the age of the dying parents, my friends and I confide in each other. Some go suddenly without any warning. Some go after a lengthy agony of distress and weariness. Some go at a gradual pace of overall weakening. It is a blessing to be able to 'go gentle into that good night', to walk towards eternity.

What eternity holds we don't know, when we shuffle to that 'undiscovered country from whose bourn no traveler returns'. We cannot prove there's a heaven and we cannot prove there's none. Everyone has their own belief, conviction or idea about what lies beyond, including the one who is sure that there's nothing out there and that's the way it should be. This shows the abundant variety in people, in opinions, feelings and impressions. How peaceful it would be on Earth if we could respect each other in this matter.

Over the last few years I have become more involved in the informal care for my mother who is in her nineties now. She's still living on her own and in good health, considering her age. She doesn't take any medications which is quite unique. She has some domestic help and meals and groceries are brought to her home. Besides that, she manages herself, with a little help from her neighbours and her children. In summer, she mows the lawn herself, step by step, panting like an old workhorse.

She is forgetful but not demented. One gradually gets used to repeating stories and questions and one learns to cope with the practical side-effects of a deteriorating short-term memory. The table agenda has become indispensable. There are risks. She is unstable and has fallen a few times. One fall with a fracture of an arm, leg or hip and it's done with her independence, that's clear. So we keep our fingers crossed, say our little prayers and hope for the best. And we still very much enjoy her company.

Caregiving has its lessons for me. As a self-proclaimed Professor in Personal Development, I have my issues, my learning goals and my growing edges. I've worked in company trainings with groups of over a hundred people, but this job requires more skill, tact and zeal. It reminds me of the story of a former client of mine, a thousand-plus boss, who asserted that one who survived the board of his son's day-care could easily manage a Fortune-500 company. The great is revealed in the small. It's back to basics.

First, this is my mother. She has birthed me, fed me, raised me and loved me, all my life. Whatever I do and do not do at this time, I am forever in her debt anyway. Second, we are our parents, mainly. Genetically and developmentally, our fates are tied. One looks a little more like the father and the other a little more like the mother, but that's about it. We often do not want to see the similarities. You are just like your father, our spouse then says.

So, I am you and you are me. I recognise so many small things in the way you move, talk and handle things. I remember some from your mother, my grandmother, how she would wipe the countertop with a worn-out cloth. I see that you peel an apple precisely how I would do it. I notice your self-will and resolve. I am not like that at all yet have been accused all my life of the same vice. When I sit, I drum with my fingers, just like you.

This is the last episode of our life together and it is a special time, a godsend. A gift that comes with life-lessons and so it's a real gift. You were the first mirror in my life and I may be your last. You perceive your future in me and through your eyes I look into eternity. We are both aware that this is a time of parting, yet we live and talk as if we could be living forever. There is an undercurrent of both sadness and joyfulness.

You show me how to die as you once taught me how to walk. The latest thing I learned about dying consciously is that presence slowly fades away. Given time and health, it is a sheer wonder of life that you have been granted this chance of passing. We are all passers-by. You may be closer to passing over and one day you will have passed away. I cannot quite feel the pain within that is caused by this slow farewell. Maybe it hurts more than I can see.

We may not easily associate personal development with the process of dying. Here comes help from beyond, however, to build our character, to learn important life-lessons, to feel real appreciation and to emphasise relativity in the light of matters of life and death. This learning may soften the edges, silence us or calm us down. It may withhold us from dumb decisions about more, better, faster and higher. These are all extraordinary insights and experiences, neither taught nor caught at a personal development seminar. Death is the ultimate teacher.

When you take care of the elderly, could be a parent, could be a neighbour, you are opening yourself up to the influence of what lies beyond for yourself. They are living in a world that is yet to come for you. In our culture we're not too keen on that. Maybe you think it's only about ageing and dying, about loss and decay, not the sort of stuff you prefer to think about on your day off or in your well-deserved, peaceful weekend. Isn't there something more exciting?

But this is a misconception. You surely don't think only fun things are meaningful. What happens when you contact the elderly, when you spend time with them, when you assist and listen to them, is that your soul becomes acquainted with a next phase in life. And that is a good preparation. Your soul likes that. There is nothing wrong about ageing. People do it all the time. One just moves on to a next phase and each phase has its pros and cons. Nothing to be afraid of.

You may have to practise patience and deepen your listening skills, but it is a good meditation practice to sit or walk with the elderly and to stay with them for some time. Then a secret transmission starts up and it flows from the elderly to those who are younger. It is a calming, slowing, grounding energy and it only works when you allow yourself to be present with it for a certain amount of time and with a certain regularity. This is what the elderly offer in exchange.

By spending time with the generations before you that are still alive, you also connect to the generations before you that are no longer alive. This works the strongest within your own family lineage. Ancestor worship has been for decades (and maybe for centuries) a declining business in the West. People think it's superstition, at best. They either believe that the dead are dead and, besides a striking portrait, there is nothing there to gain or they believe that it is even dangerous to mess with such spiritistic baloney.

Most other cultures in the world would disagree. Reverence for ancestors may influence your life in a good way, 1.5 billion Chinese know. Ancestor worship refers to rituals designed to commemorate and venerate the spirits of one's deceased forebears. The social or non-religious function of ancestor worship is to cultivate kinship values such as filial piety, family loyalty and continuance of the family lineage. Filial piety (from Latin *filialis*, meaning from a son or daughter) primarily implies to be good to one's parents and to take care of them.

Paradise lies under the feet of your mother, my local Islamic grocer recited. I am starting to understand what he means. To reach her feet, I have to bow, thereby showing her respect. To touch the ground under her feet, implies to touch the earth, thereby showing respect to all that came before her and returned to dust. I feel very blessed that my mother is still around. She is a kindred spirit with a unique personality and has lived an exceptional and eventful life. May God bless her.

THE KNOWING FIELD

Imagine a big circle of people, sitting on chairs. On one chair in the circle, a facilitator is sitting with, on the right, a client. The client is explaining a situation from childhood and mentions the persons involved. Then, the client asks a few people out of the circle to stand up to represent these persons. The facilitator suggests placing the representatives somewhere within the circle, relative to one another, in a way that mirrors the client's inner image of the childhood situation described. And so it is done.

The facilitator stands up and asks the representatives how they are doing, being part of the client's past situation. The representative for the mother is feeling wobbly, she doesn't stand firm, she explains. The representative for the father was placed turned away from the others. He says he doesn't belong here. He is staring in the distance, looking aloof. The representative for the sister stands next to the mother and she is fine. The representative for the client spontaneously mentions a feeling of tightness, having little room to manoeuvre.

Seeing this and hearing this, the client is moved to tears and shares that this is exactly how it was in this family. The father apparently had been forced into marriage. Next, the facilitator invites the representative of the father to follow any urge to move and he immediately moves to the side of the circle. The representative of the client then wishes to move next to the mother. This being done, the representative of the mother reports that she is standing firmer now, with both children close by.

This is an example from the practice of family constellations, originally developed by German family therapist Bert Hellinger at the beginning of the new century. I was so taken by this method that I followed Hellinger around the world for some years, participating in several multi-day workshops. Observing this work, one of the first questions people always ask is: how can it be that the representatives are able to know so perfectly what has actually happened in this family? Representatives say that participation feels natural without acting or interpreting.

To explain this phenomenon, Albrecht Mahr, a German medical doctor and psychotherapist, came up with the term 'the knowing field' (Mahr, 1999). Apparently, there is a wide energetic realm in this world, covering space and time, to which one may attune. Given the right position in the right circumstances, one can actually access this energetic field and retrieve 'information' from it. Not in a rational, mental sense but by intuition, by feeling, by instinct. The proper awareness and understanding become available when one is part of this knowing field.

The famous biologist Rupert Sheldrake has been involved in this work too. He is widely known for his scientific hypothesis of morphic resonance, a process whereby self-organising systems inherit a memory from previous similar systems (Sheldrake, 1988). During my first workshop with Hellinger, in London in 2000, I found myself standing in a constellation on a stage opposite a somehow familiar face, Rupert Sheldrake. Me, a representative for a Balkan general, and he, for a victim of war. Hellinger and Sheldrake manufactured a video together, titled *Re-Viewing Assumptions* (2000).

Another, ancient, understanding of the knowing field comes from the Native Americans (or First Nation) tradition. *Mitakuye Oyasin* (All Are Related) is a saying from the Lakota language. The creed reflects the world view of interconnectedness held by the Lakota people. This concept and phrase, also known as 'All My Relations', is expressed in many Yankton Sioux prayers as well as by ceremonial people in other Lakota communities. The ability to move into an informative trance has been known by all traditional medicine men and women since time immemorial.

I feel this is similar to the Jungian notion of the collective unconscious and the philosophical concepts of *anima mundi* (world soul) and *unus mundus* (one soul). The last two phrases have a rich history in Western philosophy, going back as far as Plato. The thought that humanity has always been tapping into an available greater intelligence and wisdom is to be honest (and hopefully without sounding pretentious or snobbish) entirely logical to me. I have always 'known' stuff I couldn't possibly know, thus earning the nickname The Alchemist.

'With great power comes great responsibility'. This adage comes from Peter Parker in *Spider-Man*, although, apparently, it can be traced back to 1793, to the French Revolution. An Islamic parallel has been traditionally attributed to the Prophet Muhammad: 'All of you are shepherds and each of you is responsible for his flock'. A Christian parallel from Jesus is told in Luke 12:48: 'For everyone to whom much is given, from him much will be required; and to whom much has been committed, of him they will ask the more'.

I feel, in this day and age, we absolutely need this connection to an extended field of intelligence. Many ancient sources of wisdom have been uncovered and brought to our awareness over the last decades. This book (as do my previous ones) recounts many of these traditional sources of health. I feel blessed and excited that I am living in this era and have had the chance to get to know these old yet new systems and instruments for they have brought understanding of and healing to my wounds.

For the last half century or so, we have been trying to work with these refined, rediscovered methods. This hasn't been an easy process. We have been given mighty powers but do not yet know how to use them properly. We often do not have the proper attitude. We are hampered by our egos, by our desires, by our fears and by our ignorance. We make many terrible mistakes. We are like children playing with fire. When we press the wrong button, we say: Oops, I did it again!

Let me give an example from the world of the enneagram and maybe you yourself know examples from yoga, martial arts, acupuncture, breathing work, healing, shamanism, meditation, ayurveda, constellations, and so on. One of the uses of the enneagram is its typology that reveals the deeper motives of different personalities. Often today, the enneagram is used to judge, hurt, spite, frighten or box-in people. Even in the steaming room of the sauna last week, someone demeaned an accidental absent guest by exclaiming that this was a terrible enneagram type.

We must be lenient in our judgements of others (me included, in the last paragraph). Yet, we must also correct each other, in a respectful and friendly way, in case of misuse of these wonderful instruments for personal development. Without kind and honest feedback, the process of learning to work with our new tools will take much longer. It may take years before the teething troubles will be over. At the same time we have help from beyond. The knowing field has an incredible healing power to be deployed.

I have the impression that we are often balanced out by our own process. If we go off or too far, we lose connection with our heart and soul and then there's inner work to be done. This is the advantage of spiritual work. It cannot be faked or falsified because the nature of the work is anchored in truth and love. Without love, we lose our friends and clients. Without truth, they won't come back for our support and advice. True spiritual friends dare to confront each other.

It has been three years since the corona plague started to scourge our planet. The infections have quietened down but we are still amidst its enormous economic, militaristic and relational aftermath. We have all had a huge hammer blow. The first responses are usually denial, defence and defection. This happened right after. Ranging from back to normal, blaming others and backing off. Spiritually, we all had to take quite a setback. Compassionately acknowledging this is the second step to take. This way, a process of tender healing is initiated.

We cannot do without the knowing field anymore. Attuning could become a daily routine, a way of life. I think the poet Rainer Maria Rilke knew that the knowing field is also known as God, when he wrote:

It seems
my God is dark
and like a web: a hundred roots
silently drinking.

This is the ferment I grow out of.

More I don't know, because my branches
rest in deep silence, stirred only by the wind.

Rilke's Book of Hours, I.3
Translation A. Barrows & J. Macy, 1996.

BEHOLD, THE LAMB OF GOD

When the Host is distributed during the Eucharist in De Papagaai, the Roman Catholic Church of St. Joseph on Kalverstraat in Amsterdam, the gathered faithful, mostly a handful of solitary elderly, shuffle up the aisle to the front and kneel all in unison on a wide red-clad kneeler (before the partition between the nave and the choir) that extends across the entire width of the choir. They stretch out both hands, left over right, palms up, to receive a minuscule part of the holy, consecrated, transubstantiated Body of Christ.

The officiating priest then walks up and down the partition, delivering wafers, one by one, into the hands of the yearning faithful. Some traditional Catholics, mostly women but apparently also South Americans (this I have noticed), do not stretch out their combined hands, but they stick their head forward, mouth wide open, tongue far out, upon which the celebrant then tenderly deposits the Host, affirmatively whispering the words: The Body of Christ. Thus, a whole row of humbly kneeling believers is served more or less at the same time.

When a friend of mine, who was raised without a trace of religion, once received the Host during Holy Mass on Christmas Eve in our student town Groningen, he did not immediately swallow the wafer but kept it in his hand. As he was leaving the church, an old woman came up to him, murmuring indignantly: Where are you taking the Body of the Lord? My memory does not recall whether or not he swallowed this, to him, meaningless piece of bread after all, if only to reassure her.

The sight of this entire line of devotees at Holy Communion in the Parrot Church in Amsterdam reminds me of the moment of feeding the goats at my sister and brother-in-law's goat farm in Spain. The animals gather around the trough, the manger, always hungry, seemingly starving, being totally dependent for their nourishment on what the shepherd will provide. I sometimes imagine the believers in the chapel starting to push and shove each other, with headbutts and bodychecking, to snatch the first, the best and most of the wafers.

This image is maybe not as ludicrous as you think. In our busy society, many people complain about the spiritual emptiness of their lives, craving for meaning, connection and love, and many people are miserably hungry for deliverance, redemption and salvation. I have sat in that pew more than once praying my heart out to a distant, unreachable, void image of God, lost in anguish and misery. I cannot be the only one. 'The mass of men lead lives of quiet desperation' which most people are afraid to admit.

For many years, I have been intrigued by the phenomenon of the Eucharist or Holy Communion in the Catholic Church. Being a Protestant by birth, baptised and brought up, the Catholic faith always had a strange attraction. At elementary school in Bible belt Holland, it was imprinted upon our pure souls that there was something fundamentally wrong with Catholics. When I ended up living in Amsterdam, a purely Catholic city and historically even a place of pilgrimage, fate or destiny placed the burden upon me to check this fact.

In 1996, I participated in the Eucharist at Holy Mass at the Sacré-Coeur Basilica in Paris. I tried to participate, I should say, for I was refused. At that time, one had to be Catholic to be allowed to partake. I didn't care, joined the line and, coming to the celebrant, this shrewdly peeking inquisitor hissed: Vous êtes Catholique? Are you Catholic? Completely taken aback, I muttered, in honesty: Non. No. Whereupon the agent of God judged: C'est pas pour vous. It's not for you. I drifted off, defeated.

In 2012, I had my revenge, again at the Sacré-Coeur. This time, I had sworn I would lie before God would the question be asked again, but I was lovingly welcomed. I am joking about it, yet I feel sincere. Something happens to me during this ritual. Some readers may think I am exaggerating, but I really have come to feel that the miracle of blood and wine is actually taking place at the moment of consecration. Something inside me is stilled and I sometimes sense a holy presence.

With reverence, I look at the altar. This is a wondrously holy and sacred yet, at the same time, a cruel and dreadful object. It's a normal table, yes, but its history goes back to the Jewish people who used the altar as a place for offerings to God. For centuries, the burnt offering was a twice-daily animal sacrifice, offered on the altar in the temple in Jerusalem until it was entirely consumed by fire. By killing the animal, forgiveness and redemption were sought. Sacrifice as payment for reconciliation.

Then came Jesus. He offered to make the whole offering affair obsolete with one grand gesture. Take me. Kill me. Behold, the Lamb of God, that taketh away the sin of the world. By sacrificing the Son of God all other offerings would from then on be superfluous. At the Last Supper, Jesus' rehearsal dinner, he showed his disciples, in miniature, what was going to happen. He would put himself on the altar. He would let his flesh be pierced and his blood be spilled. He would be butchered.

Each Monday morning, I do my groceries for the week. When I enter my regular neighbourhood supermarket, the butcher in the back of the shop has already put a glass of

Moroccan tea on the counter for me. He and his brother, the grocer, greet me kindly. We chat and we joke. I intend to skip the meat displays, but sometimes the temptation is too harsh. I love a fine piece of meat. I love falafel too and I am wild about the olives, the feta and the tomatoes.

In the very back of the shop stands a sturdy, daily used and worn slaughtering-table on which the butcher cuts and slices his meats into pieces with his knives and choppers. The meat is cheaper here because the entire animal is used. I can attest that this man loves his job, loves his meat and loves his clients. The altar in the Parrot Church on Kalver-straat is a slaughtering-table too. At each Holy Commun-ion, this table commemorates the butchering, the slaugh-ter, the offering and the sacrifice of Jesus Christ.

The blood and the wine together form such a powerful symbol. They refer to our basic survival instinct, eating by killing. The ancient rituals of offering - found all over the world and meant to worship, please and pay-off an exten-sive variety of deities - return in their transformed, refined and spiritualised meaning. You need to sacrifice something valuable in order to achieve something more valuable. You need to give up a lower desire in favour of a higher desire. You need to restrain an instinct to acquire goodness.

This is so deep, so profound, so essential, so beautiful, so moving, so humbling, so stilling. I look at the alter and I see the priest lift up his arm with a shiny blade in his hand. It trembles in the air. Then it comes down with the force of a hammer. It cuts into the flesh. Blood splashes about and gushes from the open wound. *Agnus Dei, qui tollis pecca-ta mundi, miserere nobis.* Lamb of God, who takes away the sin of the world, have mercy on us.

The priest lifts both hands and holds up a round wafer. He mumbles a prayer and bows. The congregation bows in response. Then he lifts the chalice and again mumbles a prayer. Priest and congregation bow in unison. This is the Holy Moment. Something in me settles. I feel very small and very quiet. I feel I am close to a mystery. I sense the reverent silence of the congregation. I feel the quietness and stillness within are calming me to accept the hardest circumstances in my daily life.

When I lift my tea glass, I say: *Shukran*. Thank you. The butcher is cleaning behind the counter. He smiles. I don't understand his reply. After fifteen years, I only know five words of Arabic. This is the start of my working week. I come to receive and to offer, strength and encouragement. In food and in words. In goods and in gesture. When I have put my groceries in my basket, I walk to the check-out. I pay and say goodbye. *Ma'a salama*. With safety, with peace. Goodbye.

DEAD MAN'S BOOTS

This is the last chapter of what is possibly my last book in the English language. When I started book V, I looked at my notes on topics to write about and before me I saw the jumble of possible themes, unrefined ideas and sudden brainwaves fall into three distinct categories: the sexes, the West and The Great Beyond. In the years after, I found no reason to change this sequence. Besides, with professional help, I designed and constructed a slipcase, to store and preserve exactly seven thin books.

Many years ago, a family member handed me a large plastic bag with old books and cahiers which apparently had belonged to my long deceased father. The bag supposedly contained a collection on esotericism and occultism. I myself am always reluctant to venture into areas of spiritism and sorcery. I am sure such powers do exist but something deep within me keeps me from moving in that direction. It might be fear; it might be intuition. I have always been attracted to spirituality, as I hope to have shown.

I have never opened the large plastic bag. Still I feel I walk in my father's footsteps by writing these seven books. I don't 'see' him or perceive his presence, but I imagine he would be proud of me knowing I have been working on matters of spirituality and religion and always, I hope, from a practical viewpoint, looking for application and implementation. Pop musician Sting wrote a song, 'Dead Man's Boots', about receiving the old working boots of his father and his reluctance to try them on himself.

The son wants to find his own way and, at some point, doesn't want to continue on the path his father laid out for him. It is the clash between generations, the confrontation of father and son, a natural, common and needed encounter to find personal strength, direction and conviction. My father died when I was just seven. I know now, from my work on life-phases (my green book II), that, at seven, a boy normally moves from the world of the mother to the world of the father.

I could not make this move. There were some replacement figures in my youth, but, basically, I have struggled with the early loss of my father all my life. A certain part of the music I have composed so far (piano & lyrics, under the artist name of Aran York) can be viewed as an artistic processing of this personal drama. The bond had been cut and nothing could replace it. Everybody has a holy wound in life and this is mine. And it has been an inspiration too.

Paul McCartney lost his mother, Mary, of cancer when he was fourteen years old. A year later, he met his musical soul mate John Lennon. They began making music together. Another year later, John's mother, Julia, was killed in a car accident. He was seventeen years old. After that, the two motherless boys became the leaders and main composers of the world's greatest pop group ever. Loss is not what we look for, but it acquires a meaning in our lives. We learn to create from our holy wound.

This may all sound rather mature and grounded, but I still have many issues to work with as you may have read between the lines in this book and as my friends can undoubtedly attest. I have never been married and have no children of my own. Sometimes I feel my books are a legacy to the son I never had. And that's okay too. My life is very beautiful and fulfilling, even without a family of my own. I feel writing has brought me closer to my dad.

We take our place in the lineage of our family. We take our place in the circle of life. For many people this involves having children themselves, raising them and seeing them having children of their own. This realisation actually suffices. We don't really need thoughts about higher beings or higher powers. It would be enough to walk the dog at night and look at the stars, feeling contented about one's life, including all hardships and losses. And including the loss of one's own life whenever this may occur.

We don't need words to describe The Great Beyond. We don't need thoughts about the beyond or an afterlife. There's no need to concern ourselves with those matters. The present, our immediate environment, our inner journey, that is enough. Possibly wordless, possibly thoughtless. But never without awareness, without consciousness, without presence. Being present is the only job we have. A wonder out of respect for ourselves, for our innate value, for our beingness. Present with whatever comes by in our minds, hearts and lives. An alert and active presence.

When we lose the unneeded thoughts about our current life and situation, we become clearer in our minds and hearts and we have more openness, energy and focus for what lies in front of us. This process of emptying our mind can be enhanced by our spiritual work on ignorance, desire and fear. Reading good books and having a practice group or a wise teacher, can alleviate ignorance. Not all at once, but gradually. Meditation is a way to awaken, to sink deeper into the truth about the world.

Seeing through our illusions, attachments and misbeliefs unveils reality without distortions. It is very well possible to attain this state. I need to say this because we have been educated in the belief that there is no objective truth. All perception would be subjective and we would all have our personal truth. This is not true. It is a manifestation of ignorance. Once you see, feel and sense the truth of the present moment, you have come home and although you may lose it again, you know it exists.

Part of the objective truth is carefulness, compassion and change. So don't be afraid you will become an insufferably rigid and cocky preacher. Working on your desires is the hardest part. Here you encounter all your attachments to what you think you really need. This is the Buddha's domain: desire is the root of all suffering. You gradually make the change from false desires to heart desires. Finally, fear becomes your focus of inquiry. Essentially, all untruth arises from fear. Fear creates false desires and false desires create ignorance.

Where there is fear there cannot be love. A reverend in the church of my youth said this in a sermon, years ago. With my dearest mother I was sitting in a pew, a few rows behind where I used to sit with my family, next to my father. According to proper Protestant tradition, my father used to give me a peppermint before the dull, lengthy sermon began, but before he handed it to me, he cracked it in two with his thumb in the palm of his hand.

I had no fear, sitting next to my dad. Awe, perhaps. Respect, for sure. But no fear. I completely trusted his presence, his nearness, his warmth. I felt safe and held, protected and cared for. Not with these words, I was seven years old. However long the tedious sermon would last, I sat there close to my dad and my thoughts could wander off freely. As long as I would not wiggle too much, everything would be fine. This was a timeless, eternal moment, beyond history, barriers and death.

Maybe we'll meet again, some sunny day. For those of you who have followed me through seven books in seven years, I take off my hat and I bow to you. It's been more than a pleasure to have talked to you, entertained you and, hopefully, inspired you. I've received quite some feedback through the years, criticism and appreciation. Friends have ignored my work; friends have cherished my work. Maybe I will continue to write in Dutch. And non-Dutch readers?

Who knows… Google Translate is getting better and better…

Arriving at the end, I would like to mention Rosemary Cowan, my first editor (four books), and Carien Heldring, my loyal pre-reader. Likewise, I would like to mention Jan de Groot, designer, and Angus Clark, editor (three books, including this one). It has been so good to work with you. My best wishes for the protection of the people, the peace, the planet. My best wishes for you, dear reader, may you proceed with care, joy and stamina. I am going to take a walk now, through the woods.

Gert Jurg, Amsterdam, 25 January 2023

Not alike a king, but like an
actor, he throws on, instead of
that splendid cloak, a grey one –
and he draws back unnoticed.

Plutarch – *Life of Demetrios*

Printed in Great Britain
by Amazon